Basic English Usage
Exercises

Without Key

Jennifer Seidl
Michael Swan

Oxford University Press

Oxford University Press
Walton Street, Oxford OX2 6DP

Oxford   New York   Toronto
Delhi Bombay   Calcutta   Madras   Karachi
Petaling Jaya   Singapore   Hong Kong   Tokyo
Nairobi   Dar es Salaam   Cape Town
Melbourne   Auckland

and associated companies in
Beirut   Berlin   Ibadan   Nicosia

OXFORD is a trade mark of Oxford University Press.

ISBN 0 19 431189 9

© Oxford University Press 1986

First published 1986
Without key edition 1987
Second impression 1987

Cartoons by Marie-Hélène Jeeves
Other illustrations by Katey Farrell, Alan Suttie
Photographs by Rob Judges, Terry Williams

The publishers would like to thank Hertz, Daimler-
Benz AG, British Telecom and the International Wool
Secretariat for permission to use trade marks and
copyright material, and Barnabys, Camera Press, Rex
Features for permission to reproduce photographs.

Typeset by Tradespools Ltd, Frome, Somerset

Printed in Hong Kong

Contents

Introduction   3

List of Exercises   4

Exercises   7–100

Introduction

General

This book of exercises was written to accompany Michael Swan's *Basic English Usage*, but it can also be used on its own. It provides practice and revision material on over 200 important points of usage, grammar and lexis. It is intended for students of English from lower intermediate level upwards and is suitable both for use in class and for self study.

Exercises

The 230 exercises are varied in approach to suit the topic and the needs of the user. With few exceptions, the exercises are contextualized. Many exercises make use of picture cues. Several exercises are controlled, i.e. they have a limited number of possible answers. Others are open-ended, i.e. they offer freer communicative practice. Here the student is guided towards expressing wishes, preferences, opinions, etc within the framework of a specific language item. The student relates to and draws on his personal situation, own background and experience.

Organization

The language points treated are dealt with alphabetically, as in *Basic English Usage*. In the vast majority of cases, each exercise deals with one *BEU* point only. This makes the exercise book very easy to use together with *Basic English Usage*. All exercises are cross-referenced to the corresponding sections of *Basic English Usage* and most have at least one example.

Key

Basic English Usage: Exercises is published in two editions, one with a Key and one without. The Key contains the answers to all the exercises.
Where the exercise is open-ended, suggestions are made or examples of possible answers are given.

List of Exercises

1 **about to** (BEU 2)
2 **above** and **over** (3)
3 **across, over, through** (4, 5)
4 adverbs: position (14)
5 adverbs: indefinite frequency (14.2)
6 adverbs: indefinite frequency (14.2)
7 adverbs of manner (14.6)
8 adverbs: position (place, time) (14.9)
9 **after** (preposition); **afterwards** (adverb) (16)
10 **ago** (20)
11 **all** (21–24)
12 **although** (29)
13 **another** (33)
14 articles: **the, a/an** (40,41)
15 articles: special rules and exceptions (45)
16 articles: special rules and exceptions (45)
17 articles: **a/an** (45.6)
18 **as . . . as** (46)
19 **as** and **like** (48)
20 **as, when** and **while** (52.1)
21 **ask** (53)
22 **at, in** and **on** (place) (54)
23 **at, in** and **on** (place) (54)
24 **at, in** and **on** (time) (55)
25 **be** + infinitive (58)
26 **because** and **because of** (60)
27 **before** (conjunction) (62)
28 **before** (preposition) and **in front of** (63)
29 **big, large, great** and **tall** (65)
30 **borrow** and **lend** (67)
31 **both** with verbs (69)
32 **bring** and **take** (71)
33 **can** and **could**: ability (78.1)
34 **can**: ability (78.2)
35 **could**: ability (78.3)
36 **can**: possibility (79)
37 **can**: possibility (79.1)
38 **could have**: probability (79.3)
39 **can**: permission, offers (80.1,3)
40 **could/couldn't**: past permission (80.2)
41 **come** and **go** (83)
42 comparison: comparative adjectives (84)
43 comparison: superlative adjectives (84)
44 comparison: superlative adjectives (85.5)
45 comparison: **much, far** etc with comparatives (86)
46 conditional: progressive conditional (88.1)
47 conditional: use (88.2a)
48 conjunctions (89.3)
49 'copula' verbs (91)
50 countable and uncountable nouns (92)
51 dates (95)
52 dates (95.2)
53 **do**: auxiliary verb (98.1,2)
54 **do** + **-ing** (99)
55 **do** and **make** (100)
56 **during** and **for** (101)
57 **during** and **in** (102)
58 **each other** and **one another** (105)
59 **else** (109)
60 emphatic structures with **it** (111)
61 **enjoy** (112)
62 **enough** (113.1)
63 **enough** (113.2)
64 **enough** (113.3)
65 **even though** (114.4)
66 **ever** (116)
67 **except** and **except for** (119)
68 exclamations (120.1,2)
69 **explain** (123)

70 **fairly, quite, rather** and **pretty** (124)
71 **far** and **a long way** (125)
72 **farther** and **further** (126)
73 **(a) few** and **(a) little** (129)
74 **(a) few** and **(a) little** (129)
75 **fewer** and **less** (130)
76 **fewer** and **less** (130)
77 **for**: purpose (131.1)
78 **for**: purpose (131.2)
79 **for** + object + infinitive (132.1)
80 **for** + object + infinitive (132.1)
81 **for** and **since** (133.1–3)
82 **for** and **since** (133.4)
83 future: present progressive (135.1)
84 future: **going to** (135.2)
85 future: **going to** (135.2)
86 future: **shall/will** (predictions) (136)
87 future: **shall/will** (predictions) (136)
88 future: simple present (138.1)
89 future perfect (139)
90 future perfect (139)
91 future progressive (140)
92 **get** + noun/pronoun/adjective (142.1,2)
93 **go: been** and **gone** (145.1)
94 **go** meaning 'become' (146.2)
95 **go . . . -ing** (147)
96 **had better** (148)
97 **hard** and **hardly** (150)
98 **have**: possession etc (153.1)
99 **have (got)**: possession etc (153.2)
100 **have**: actions (154)
101 **have** + object + past participle (155.2)
102 **have** + object + past participle (155.2)
103 **have (got) to** (156)
104 **have (got) to** (156)
105 **hear** and **listen (to)** (157)
106 **home** (161)
107 **if**: ordinary tenses (164.1)
108 **if**: special tenses (165.1)
109 **if**: special tenses, present and future situations (165.1)
110 **if**: special tenses, past situations (165.3)
111 **if**: special tenses, past situations (165.3)
112 **if**-sentences with **could** (166)
113 **if only** (167)
114 imperative (170)
115 imperative (170.1)
116 imperative: with **do** (170.1)
117 **in case** (172.1,2)
118 **in spite of** (173)
119 infinitive: verb + object + infinitive (176.3)
120 infinitive: verb + object + infinitive (176.3)
121 infinitive after **who, what, how** etc (177.1)
122 infinitive of purpose (178)
123 infinitive of purpose (178)
124 infinitive of purpose (178)
125 **-ing** form ('gerund') (180.2)
126 **-ing** form ('gerund') after verb (180.3)
127 **-ing** form ('gerund') after **need** and **want** (180.4)
128 **-ing** form ('gerund') after preposition (180.5)
129 **-ing** form or infinitive? (182.1)
130 irregular verbs (186)
131 **it's time** (189.2)
132 **let's** (191)
133 **look (at), watch** and **see** (196)
134 **may** and **might**: probability (199)
135 **may** and **might**: possibility (199)
136 **may**: permission (200.1)
137 **much, many, a lot** etc (205.1)
138 **must**: obligation (208)
139 **must**: obligation (208)
140 **must**: deduction (210.1,2)

141 **must**: deduction (210.3)
142 nationality words (212)
143 nationality words (212)
144 nationality words (212)
145 nationality words (212)
146 nationality words (212)
147 **need** (213)
148 **neither** (217.1)
149 **neither ... nor ...** (218)
150 **next** and **nearest** (219)
151 **no** and **none** (221)
152 **no** and **not** (222)
153 numbers (227.1)
154 numbers (227.4)
155 numbers (227.5)
156 numbers (227.6)
157 numbers (227.7)
158 numbers (227.8)
159 numbers (227.2,3,9)
160 numbers (227.10)
161 numbers (227.2,12)
162 **one**: substitute word (230)
163 **ought** (232)
164 **ought to have** (232.4)
165 **own** (233.2)
166 participles used as adjectives (235)
167 participle clauses (236)
168 passive verb forms: simple present (238)
169 passive verb forms: simple present (238)
170 passive verb forms: present progressive (238)
171 passive verb forms: simple past (238)
172 passive verb forms: simple past (238)
173 passive verb forms: present perfect (238)
174 passive verb forms: future perfect (238)
175 passive verb forms: '**going to**' (238)
176 past time: simple past (241)
177 past time: past progressive (242)
178 past time: present perfect simple (243.3)
179 past time: present perfect simple (243.4,5)
180 past time: present perfect progressive (244.2)
181 past perfect simple (245)
182 possessive **'s** (250.1)
183 possessive **'s** (250.4)
184 possessive **'s** (250.4)
185 possessives with determiners (**a friend of mine** etc) (252)
186 possessives: **mine** etc (253.2)

187 prepositions at the end of clauses (257.1d)
188 present tenses: simple present (261.2)
189 present tenses: present progressive (262.2)
190 present tenses: present progressive (262.2)
191 progressive tenses with **always** (263)
192 questions (270)
193 question tags (273)
194 reflexive pronouns (276.2)
195 relative pronouns: **who** (277)
196 relative pronouns: **that** (277.2)
197 relatives: **whose** (279)
198 relatives: identifying clauses (280)
199 reported speech: tenses (283.3)
200 reported speech: tenses (283.3)
201 reported speech: questions (284)
202 reported speech: questions (284)
203 reported speech: orders, requests, advice etc (285)
204 **the same** (288)
205 **shall** (292.2)
206 short answers (293.1)
207 short answers (293.2)
208 **should** (294)
209 **should** (294.2)
210 **since** (conjunction of time): tenses (300)
211 spelling of plural nouns (301)
212 **so** and **not** with **hope**, **believe** etc (311)
213 **so am I**, **so do I** etc (312)
214 **some** and **any** (314)
215 **somebody** and **anybody**, **something** and **anything** etc (317)
216 **still**, **yet** and **already** (330)
217 subject and object forms (331.1)
218 **such** and **so** (334)
219 **take** (time) (338)
220 telling the time (342.1,2)
221 **there is** (345.1)
222 **until** and **by** (351); **until** and **to** (352)
223 **used to** + infinitive (353)
224 **(be) used to** + **...-ing** (354)
225 verbs with two objects (356.1)
226 **when** and **if** (360), **whether** and **if** (351); (361)
227 **whoever**, **whatever**, **whichever**, **however**, **whenever** and **wherever** (365)
228 **wish** (367.2)
229 **worth ... -ing** (368)
230 **would rather** (370.2)

men/are

1 **about to** (BEU 2)

What are they all about to do?

▶ *The policeman's **about to** stop the traffic.* (1)

policeman is

1

2 *overtake*

3

4 *board*

5

6

7

8 *cross*

9 *ride*

10

11

2 **above** and **over** (BEU 3)

above, over or *both*?

I'm a student and I have a room in London. The house is *over* a hundred years old, so my room's cheap but shabby. In the corner there's a bed with a red cover *over* it. *Above* the bed there's a shelf for books. There's a crack in the wall *above* the fire-place, so I've stuck a poster __5__ it. Just *above* the crack there's a hole, so I've put a photo of my girlfriend *over* that. There's a broken mirror *above* the wash-basin, and just *above* that there's a light that doesn't work. But the room's wonderful for parties! Last night I had *over* twenty friends here. It really doesn't matter if anything gets broken!

3 **across, over, through** (BEU 4, 5)

across, over or *through*?

We live in a farmhouse in the country. When you get off the bus, you have to walk __1__ the village, __2__ the square, __3__ the narrow streets and __4__ the market-place to the church. Then you turn left and go __5__ the bridge. Don't jump __6__ the stream – it's deep! Walk __7__ the wood and __8__ the ploughed field. There's a fence round it, but you can jump __9__ that. You'll see the farmhouse from the top of the hill. If the gate's locked, just climb __10__ the wall – I always do.

4 adverbs: position (BEU 14)

Copy the story, putting the adverbs in the correct position.

7

certainly → She glanced at her watch - 2.30 am. But it had been a lovely party. She had for- *completely* gotten the time. She turned the key in *quietly* the door. But how strange - it wasn't *even* *really* locked. Had she forgotten to lock the *perhaps* door? She had. A strange feeling came *nevertheless* *suddenly* over her. Her heart started beating. She *loudly* *nervously* pushed the door open and listened. She *upstairs* heard a noise. It had come from the bed- *definitely* *at first* room. She didn't know what to do. There *obviously* was someone in the house. She must think *clearly* what to do. She knew that she must ring *at once* the police. She moved towards the phone. *silently* *then* She remembered that it was out of order. *the morning before* She had tried to phone her brother. *unfortunately* She groped her way back to the door. There *on the hall table* was a china vase. She brushed against it

5 adverbs: indefinite frequency (BEU 14.2)

What's the weather like? Answer these questions about the weather in your country.
Use: *always*, *never*, *often*, *sometimes*, *occasionally* and *rarely* in complete sentences.

▶ Is it hot in summer?
*Yes, it's **always** hot in summer.*

Is there snow in August?
*No, there's **never** snow in August.*

1 Is there ever snow in winter?
2 Is it ever foggy?
3 Is there heavy rainfall in summer?
4 Is it ever hotter than 30°C?
5 Are there ever thunderstorms?
6 Can you sunbathe in winter?
7 Is it humid?
8 Is the temperature ever below freezing point?
9 Are there ever floods?
10 Is there ever a hurricane in your area?

6 adverbs: indefinite frequency (BEU 14.2)

What do you do in your free time? Say:

▶ what you *often* do on Saturdays.
*On Saturdays I **often** go shopping.*

1 what you *always* do on Sundays. (Begin: *On Sundays I **always** . . .*)
2 what you *often* do after school/work.
3 what you *seldom* do during the week.
4 what you *never* do at weekends.

5 what you *frequently* do in summer.
6 what you *rarely* do in winter.
7 what you *sometimes* do on holiday.
8 what you *usually* do on Sunday mornings.
9 what you *normally* do when it rains.
10 what you *occasionally* do in the evenings.

7 adverbs of manner (BEU 14.6)

Answer these questions about yourself.

▶ Are you a good swimmer?
*Yes, I swim **well**.*
*No, I don't swim **well**./No, I swim **badly**.*

1 Are you a good cook?
2 Are you a hard worker?
3 Are you a fast learner?
4 Are you a fluent speaker of English?
5 Are you a good singer?

6 Are you a heavy smoker?
7 Are you a fast runner?
8 Are you a good dancer?
9 Are you a careful driver?
10 Are you a good tennis player?

8 adverbs: position (place, time) (BEU 14.9)

What's Jill doing this week?

▶ *She has to ring Jim at his office at lunchtime.*

Continue . . .

❦ NOTES ❦

Today
ring Jim lunchtime (office)
see Brenda 12.30 (canteen)
2.15 dentist's
5.30 pick up Roger, Kings Cross Station
7.30 jazz concert, Cavern Club

❦ NOTES ❦

Tues
afternoon, town with Sarah
disco 8pm
Wed
9.15 interview, Sun Travel Agency
8pm Central Hall, concert
Thurs Manchester, 8.15 a.m.
meet Sally about 6.30pm, airport

9 after (preposition); afterwards (adverb) (BEU 16)

What did the Parkers do in London?

▶ On Monday morning...
after visiting St. Paul's Cathedral, they took a walk through the City.
or
they visited St. Paul's Cathedral and **afterwards** they took a walk through the City.

Continue...

London, August 17–20

Mon 17: Morn.	St. Paul's Cathedral walk through city
aft.	Westminister Abbey; Houses of Parliament
even.	The Mousetrap (Agatha Christie), Chinese restaurant
Tues 18: Morn	Madame Tussaud's; the Planetarium
aft.	Windsor Castle walk through Windsor
even.	boat ride on the Thames meal at steak House
Wed 19: Morn.	shopping — Oxford Street lunch Italian restaurant
aft.	British Museum; a few beers in a nearby pub
even.	concert, Queen Elizabeth Hall, supper Indian restaurant
Thurs 20: Morn.	10 Downing Street, Hyde Park
aft.	Tate Gallery coffee-shop
even.	packed suit-cases

---

10 ago (BEU 20)

ago, for or *before*?

1981: waiter, building site	1982: office job, waiter
1983: tourist guide	1984: office job, building site

In summer 1984, last year, I did an office job __1__ six weeks. I knew the work because I had done it two years __2__. Two years __3__, in summer 1983, I worked as a tourist guide in London __4__ three months. In summer 1982, that's three years __5__, I also worked as a waiter in a London hotel. I had already been a waiter __6__ three months a year __7__, so it wasn't new to me. A year __8__, I also worked on a building site __9__ four weeks. I had worked for the same firm three years __10__.

---

11 all (BEU 21–24)

all, everybody, everything, every?

POLICEMAN   Now, please tell me __1__ you know, Madam.
MRS YOUNG   Well, when I came downstairs this morning I switched on __2__ the lights, and __3__ was in a mess! __4__ the silver was missing, pictures, money, __5__ my jewellery. They had taken __6__! They had been in __7__ drawer and cupboard.
POLICEMAN   Where was __8__ at the time?
MRS YOUNG   In bed, of course, we were __9__ asleep.
POLICEMAN   Did the neighbours hear or see anything?
MRS YOUNG   __10__ our neighbours are on holiday. __11__ goes away at this time of the year.
POLICEMAN   All right, Madam. I'll just take a look round. Thank you. That's __12__ for now.

12 **although** (BEU 29)

Rewrite with *although*.

▶ I don't sleep much, but I'm not usually tired.
***Although** I don't sleep much, I'm not usually tired.*

1 I eat a lot, but I'm not fat.
2 I get up late, but I'm seldom late for work.
3 I drink a lot of beer, but I'm never drunk.
4 I drive badly, but I've never had an accident.
5 I don't look after my car, but it runs well.
6 I spend a lot of money, but I'm not in debt.
7 I don't go to the dentist's, but my teeth are healthy.

Write about some of your bad habits. Use *although*.

13 **another** (BEU 33)

You are invited to tea with an English family. How would you ask for *another* or *some more* of the following things?
Begin: *May/Could I have. . ., please?*

cup of tea	piece of chocolate cake
sugar	apple pie
sandwich	cream
two biscuits	piece of fruit cake
milk	strawberry gâteau

14 articles: **the**, **a/an** (BEU 40, 41)

the or *a*?

POLLY   There are two people sitting near __1__ door, __2__ young man and __3__ woman. __4__ man's wearing __5__ dark raincoat and __6__ woman's got __7__ big, black bag. They look suspicious. They are watching __8__ bank across __9__ road. And there's __10__ man standing at __11__ entrance to __12__ bank...

ALICE   Do you mean __13__ man in __14__ black hat?
POLLY   Yes, he looks very suspicious.
ALICE   Well, stop playing detective and pass me __15__ sugar, please. I know him – he's __16__ bank manager!

15 articles: special rules and exceptions (BEU 45)

Answer these questions about yourself. Write complete sentences, and put in *the* if necessary.

▶ What time do you go to _____ work?
I go to work at eight o'clock.

Do you live in _____ town or in _____ country?
*I live in **the** country.*

1 What time do you go to _____ work?
2 Do you live in _____ town or in _____ country?
3 What do you eat for _____ breakfast?
4 Do you go to school/work by _____ bus, by _____ bicycle or on _____ foot?
5 Do you play _____ piano or _____ guitar?
6 Do you prefer _____ mountains or _____ sea?
7 Do you prefer to go on holiday in _____ spring or in _____ summer?
8 Do you often lie in _____ sun?
9 Have you ever been in _____ hospital?
10 How often do you watch _____ television?

16 articles: special rules and exceptions (BEU 45)

Answer these questions about your country or your town. Use *the* or no article.

▶ 1 ***The*** *Amazon*
   2 *Rio Airport*

1 Which is the longest river?
2 Which is the main airport?
3 Which is the biggest lake?
4 Which are the nearest mountains?
5 Which is the highest mountain?

6 Which is the nearest sea or ocean?
7 Which is the biggest or most important university?
8 Which is the main street in your town?
9 Which is the biggest hotel in your town?
10 Which is the nearest railway station?

17 articles: **a/an** (BEU 45.6)

What are they?

translator	electrician	author	mechanic
air hostess	secretary	architect	shop assistant
nurse	actor		

▶ *Ann's **a** secretary.*

	Ann	Pam	Mike	Jim	Jeff	Joe	Pat	Bill	Tom	Mark
works in an office	●					●			●	
sells things										●
repairs things				●	●					
uses languages		●							●	
types a lot	●		●						●	
visits customers					●	●				
works with others	●	●		●			●	●		●
sometimes works at night		●					●	●		
has a famous name			●					●		

18 as ... as (BEU 46)

Compare using *as ... as* and *not as ... as.*

▶ Jim's 16, Ben's 18 and Jack's 16.
   *Jim's **as old as** Jack, but he isn't **as old as** Ben.*

1 Mary's 160 cm tall, Pat's 160 cm and Pam's 172 cm tall.
2 Dick smokes 25 cigarettes a day, Tom 40 and Peter 25.
3 Susan works 8 hours a day, Jane 8 hours and Jill 10 hours.
4 Peter earns £160 a week, Dick earns £160 and Tom earns £190.

5 Uncle Stan weighs 88 kilos, Uncle Sam weighs 108 kilos and Uncle Dan weighs 88 kilos.
6 Susan gets up at 7.30, Jill at 6.30 and Jane at 7.30.

Write some sentences like these to compare yourself with other people.

19 **as** and **like** (BEU 48)

as or *like*?

1 You look very much _____ someone I know.
2 I worked _____ a tour guide in London for three months.
3 Mr Turner is really very nice. You don't know him _____ I do.
4 Peter can swim _____ a fish!
5 I like travelling in hot countries, _____ Nigeria or Pakistan.
6 I'm good at some things, _____ music and painting.
7 In Spain, _____ in several hot countries, shops close for a few hours around midday.
8 Polly tries to dress _____ a model, but she doesn't look quite the same.
9 This year, _____ last year, all evening classes will begin at 7.30 pm.
10 Don't try to change anything. Leave things _____ they are.

20 **as, when** and **while** (BEU 52.1)

Find beginnings and ends that go together. Begin with *as, when* or *while*.

▶ ***As/When/While** I was hanging out the washing, it started to rain.*

Beginnings
I was cleaning the floor
I was phoning my aunt
I was unlocking the car
I was running for the bus
I was pushing a trolley round the supermarket
I was looking in a shop-window
I was cooking lunch
I was putting a cake in the oven
I was turning a sharp corner
I was watching the news

Ends
I fell off my bicycle
Somebody stole my purse
The phone went dead
I dropped the keys down a drain
My hat blew off
I knocked down a stack of tins
The dog knocked over the bucket of water
The television broke down
The electricity went off
I burnt my arm

21 **ask** (BEU 53)

ask or *ask for*? Put in *for* where necessary.

1 The policeman asked me _____ my name and address.
2 I asked her _____ the salt, but she didn't hear me.
3 If you get lost, ask a policeman _____ the way.
4 I felt ill, so I asked _____ to be excused.
5 I asked _____ the flowers to be delivered to my mother's address.
6 You shouldn't ask people _____ money.
7 He asked me _____ the time, but my watch had stopped.
8 Don't forget to ask him _____ the books he promised you.
9 I asked him _____ to lend me ten pounds, but he couldn't.
10 Don't forget to ask _____ the price of that house.

22 **at**, **in** and **on** (place) (BEU 54)

Look at this list, and write down the places where you would expect to see these signs.
Answer with *at*, *in* or *on*, as in the example.

aeroplane	customs	shop
airport	garden gate	train
ambulance	Mercedes car	woollen
box	museum	clothing
cinema	park (twice)	zoo

▶ **on** *leather goods*

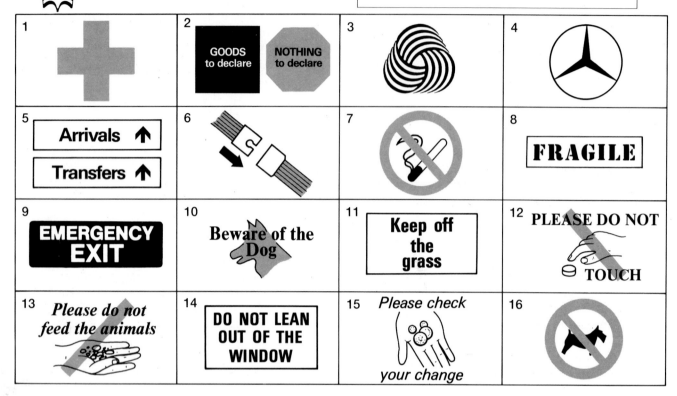

23 **at**, **in** and **on** (place) (BEU 54)

Where do you usually do some of the following things?
Use *at*, *in* or *on* and *a/the*.

▶ read the newspaper?
   at *home*, **on** *the bus*, **in** *the kitchen*, etc

1 read the newspaper?
2 shop for food?
3 keep your bicycle/car?
4 post letters?
5 watch television?
6 go dancing?
7 buy records and cassettes?
8 wash your hair?
9 wait for the bus?
10 meet your friends?

24 **at**, **in** and **on** (time) (BEU 55)

When do you usually do some of the following things?
Begin with *at*, *in* or *on*.

▶ go swimming?
   in *summer*, **at** *weekends*, **on** *Saturdays*, etc

1 go swimming?
2 read the newspaper?
3 go to bed?
4 see friends?
5 have parties?
6 have lunch?
7 receive presents?
8 visit relatives?
9 go shopping?
10 have a bath?
11 have breakfast?
12 go on holiday?

25 be + infinitive (BEU 58)

Put in the correct form of *be to*.

▶ The Queen *was to* visit New Zealand in autumn, but the trip was postponed.

1 You children _____ finish your homework before you watch television.
2 Our department _____ be moved to Edinburgh, but plans were changed at the last minute.
3 The Pope _____ visit Australia next year.
4 All competition entries _____ be submitted before 30th September.
5 The teacher said the children _____ be quiet until she came back.

6 I _____ be promoted to head of department within six months!
7 The staff _____ receive a 5 per cent rise, but they only got 3 per cent.
8 The medicine _____ be taken before meals.
9 All applicants for the job _____ be interviewed in May.
10 The examination _____ be held in May, but the date was changed to 15th June.

26 because and because of (BEU 60)

Which would you choose and why? Give as many reasons as you can.

▶ A holiday in Greece or a holiday in England?
*I would choose a holiday in Greece **because of** the good weather.*
*I would choose a holiday in Greece **because** it is warmer there.*
*I would choose a holiday in England **because of** the language.*
*I would choose a holiday in England **because** I like speaking English.*

1 A sports car or a saloon car?
2 Spaghetti and ice-cream for lunch or fruit and yoghurt?
3 A seaside holiday or a skiing holiday?
4 A big old house or a small modern house?
5 A house in the country or a flat in the city?
6 A job in your own country or a job abroad?

27 before (conjunction) (BEU 62)

What do you usually do first?

▶ clean your teeth, comb your hair?
*I usually clean my teeth **before** I comb my hair.*

1 have a shower, clean your teeth?
2 get dressed, comb your hair?
3 have breakfast, get dressed?
4 shave/put on your make-up, comb your hair?
5 put on your shoes, have breakfast?

6 have breakfast, make your bed?
7 read the newspaper, have lunch?
8 watch television, read the newspaper?
9 have supper, watch television?
10 get into bed, put out the light?

28 before (preposition) and in front of (BEU 63)

before or *in front of*?

1 I must go to the hairdresser's _____ the end of the week.
2 I've parked the car _____ the police station.
3 I couldn't see much at the theatre. There was a big fat man sitting right _____ me.
4 I arrived at the office just _____ nine.
5 I'll phone you _____ Wednesday.
6 Do you know the man who's standing _____ you?

7 We couldn't go faster. There was a lorry _____ us.
8 I've got so many things to do _____ the holidays.
9 We can't stop here. We're right _____ a 'No parking' sign.
10 Can you ring me _____ the concert?

29 big, large, great and tall (BEU 65)

How would you describe the following?
Use *big*, *large*, *great* or *tall* and a
suitable noun where necessary.

▶ Winston Churchill?
   *a **great** politician/man*

   a house with twelve rooms?
   *a **big**/**large** house*

1 Abraham Lincoln?
2 a 6-seater car?
3 a building with 30 storeys?
4 a mistake that you regretted?
5 a very good friend?

6 the USSR?
7 a very good idea?
8 a tree 30 metres high?
9 Ludwig van Beethoven?
10 a flat with six rooms?

30 borrow and lend (BEU 67)

Put in the correct form of *borrow* or *lend*.

1 Can you _____ me ten pounds until the
   weekend, please?
2 I'd like to _____ Mr Andrews' camera, but I don't
   suppose he'll want to _____ it to me.
3 Don't _____ money to Peggy! She always
   forgets to pay you back.
4 Why don't you _____ Jack's bicycle? I'm sure
   he wouldn't mind.
5 Susan Webber has _____ me her tennis racket.
   Hers is better than mine.

6 Dad, can I _____ your car for the evening?
7 _____ me your pen, will you? Mine won't write.
8 I don't like _____ things from my neighbours.
9 I can't _____ you my dictionary; I've already
   _____ it to Pamela.
10 I have a lot of figures to add up. I'll _____
   Jeremy's calculator.

31 both with verbs (BEU 69)

Compare the two brothers, using *both*.

▶ *They **both** like music.*
   *They can **both** swim.*

Continue . . .

	Jeff	Bill
likes music	×	×
can swim	×	×
is over 18	×	×
likes discos	×	
has been abroad	×	×
still goes to school		×
plays a musical instrument	×	×
hates examinations	×	×
enjoys mathematics	×	×
wants to become a doctor		×
likes dancing	×	×
can drive a car	×	×
speaks a foreign language	×	×
has a girlfriend	×	×
dislikes parties		×
can play chess	×	×

32 **bring** and **take** (BEU 71)

Put in the correct form of *bring* or *take*.

1 I've got a lot of money in my bag. I must _____ it to the bank immediately.
2 Could you _____ these letters to the post office for me?
3 John's very thoughtful. Whenever he comes, he always _____ flowers.
4 You mustn't forget to _____ these books back to the library.
5 If we go by car, we can _____ the dog with us.
6 Colin's going to _____ his new car round to show us.
7 You can _____ my dictionary home with you if you like, but please don't forget to _____ it back tomorrow.
8 Mrs Lewis said she would _____ the books to the office for me.
9 Oh dear. I forgot to _____ the car to the garage.
10 When you drive to Bristol, will you _____ me with you?

33 **can** and **could**: ability (BEU 78.1)

How well can you do these things? *Very well? Quite well? A bit? Not at all?*

▶ *I can swim **quite well**.*
*I can't speak French **at all**.*

type	use a sewing machine	cook
drive a car	dance	dive
use a pocket calculator	paint	ride a bicycle
take photographs	act	play the guitar
play table tennis	play football	speak Japanese

Say how well you can do some other things.

34 **can**: ability (BEU 78.2)

What do you think people will be able to do two hundred years from now?
Begin: *I think/don't think people/we will be able to* . . .

1 live on another planet?
2 live in space?
3 live in towns on the sea-bed?
4 build cities in the desert?
5 go on holiday to the moon?
6 fly private helicopters and small planes?
7 grow food on the sea-bed?
8 travel faster than light?

Write some other things that you think/don't think people will be able to do in two hundred years.

35 **could**: ability (BEU 78.3)

Make some sentences with *could* and *couldn't*, as in the example.

▶ *I **could** speak my own language when I was four, but I **couldn't** speak English until I was 25/started this school/etc.*

Ideas:
speak your own language/speak English
walk/talk
count to ten/do geometry
say the alphabet/read
write your name/write a letter
swim/dive
play football/play chess
boil an egg/cook a meal
ride a bicycle/drive

36 **can**: possibility (BEU 79)

How long can they live? One number in each pair shows the average life span of the animals in years. Do you know which number is correct? If not, guess! Write a sentence like this:

▶ 12 or 20 years
I think a tiger **can live** *up to 20 years.* (Correct)

12 or 20 years

15 or 20 years

6 or 10 years

20 or 25 years

2 or 5 years

20 or 40 years

17 or 25 years

40 or 100 years

12 or 18 years

50 or 70 years

24 or 34 years

37 **can**: possibility (BEU 79.1)

> He's tall and slim, wearing a dark suit, dark hat and dark tie, carrying a black briefcase. He's about 35, has short dark hair and is clean-shaven without glasses.

This is a witness's description of a bank robber. Look carefully at the police suspects. Can the robber be one of them? Work it out like this:

▶ **It can't be** X because he's over 35/too small/has got a beard, etc.

38 **could have**: probability (BEU 79.3)

You have a friend who's very careless, but lucky. Nothing serious happened in the following situations, but what could have happened?

▶ She left her luggage unattended on a platform. *Someone **could have** stolen it.*

1 She left the house and forgot to close the kitchen window.
2 She left her purse in a shop.
3 She left the house and forgot to turn off the iron.
4 She drove the car after taking four sleeping pills.
5 She left her umbrella in a restaurant.

6 She wore high heeled shoes on the icy pavement.
7 She ran outside without a coat on a very cold day.
8 She jumped into a lake although she couldn't swim.
9 She climbed up a high tree to rescue a cat.
10 She parked her car in a no-parking zone.

39 can: permission, offers (BEU 80.1,3)

Asking permission. What do you think they are saying?
Use *can*.

1

2

3

4

Making offers. What do you think they are saying?
Use *can*.

5

6

7

8

40 could/couldn't: past permission (BEU 80.2)

When Joan was a student, she had a room in London.
The landlady was very strict. She put this notice on
Joan's door. What could/couldn't she do?

▶ *Joan **couldn't** have visitors after 10 pm or on Sundays.
She **could** only make drinks in the kitchen.*

Continue . . .

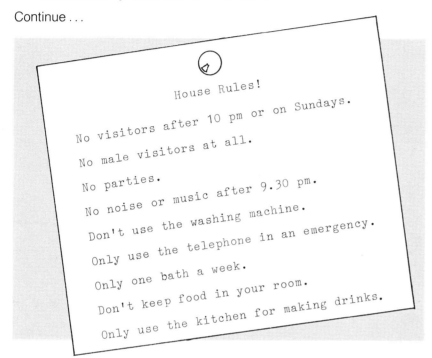

House Rules!

No visitors after 10 pm or on Sundays.

No male visitors at all.

No parties.

No noise or music after 9.30 pm.

Don't use the washing machine.

Only use the telephone in an emergency.

Only one bath a week.

Don't keep food in your room.

Only use the kitchen for making drinks.

Then write about some things that you *could/couldn't* do when you were younger.

---

41 come and go (BEU 83)

Put in the correct form of *come* or *go*.

1 Peter often _____ to visit us. We like him to _____,
but he never knows when to _____ home!
2 Shall we _____ and see Janet next weekend?
She _____ back from Edinburgh yesterday.
3 What time did you _____ to the doctor's
yesterday?
4 'Will you _____ here, please? I want to show you
something.' 'Okay. I'll _____ as soon as I can.'

5 'Can I _____ and visit you tomorrow?' 'Of
course! You're welcome to _____ any time!'
6 We _____ to Brighton yesterday. It was lovely!
7 We _____ to live in Manchester in 1965 and
we've felt very happy here.
8 Tim's five. He _____ to school now.
9 I'm _____ into hospital soon. Will you _____
and visit me?

---

42 comparison: comparative adjectives (BEU 84)

Compare yourself and your best friend.
Use comparatives of *fat, thin, dark, fair, tall, small,
young, old, cheerful, clever, intelligent, practical,
polite, musical, strong, happy.*

▶ *I'm **fatter** than he/she is.
He's/She's **more intelligent** than I am.*

43 comparison: superlative adjectives (BEU 84)

Compare the hotels using superlatives of *big*, *cheap*, *expensive*, *far*, *luxurious*, *modern*, *near*, *new*, *old*, *small*.

▶ *The Palm Beach is the **biggest***.

Hotel Atlantis ★★★★★	**Hotel Astoria** ★★★	**Hotel Palm Beach** ★★★★
● Built 1978	● Built 1970	● Built 1982
● 350 rooms	● 100 rooms	● 400 rooms
● 500m to beach	● 700m to beach	● 200m to beach
● 400m to centre	● 300m to centre	● 800m to centre
● 1 week from £334	● 1 week from £205	● 1 week from £260

44 comparison: superlative adjectives (BEU 85.5)

▶ *The Queen Elizabeth II can carry 1,800 passengers. It's the **largest** passenger ship in the world.*

Now make similar statements about the following. Use superlatives of *big*, *busy*, *cold*, *dry*, *fast*, *high*, *large*, *long*, *tall*, *wet*.

1 Egypt has only 55.8 mm of rain a year.
2 Concorde flies at a speed of approximately 2,150 k/h.
3 The Toronto Tower is 553 m tall.
4 The River Nile is 6,678 km long.
5 Antarctica has an average temperature of −60°C.
6 The Sahara Desert covers an area of 8,400,000 sq km.

7 Mount Everest is 8,848 m high.
8 Mexico City has a population of about 17 million people.
9 Colombia has as much as 4,099 mm of rain a year.
10 At Chicago International Airport a plane takes off or lands every 45 seconds.

45 comparison: **much**, **far** etc with comparatives (BEU 86)

This is a list of world temperatures on 1 September 1984. Compare the temperatures using *a lot*, *a little*, *no*, *very much* and *warmer*, *cooler*, *hotter*, *colder*, as appropriate.

▶ Las Palmas/Tenerife
*It was **a little cooler** in Las Palmas than in Tenerife.*

Edinburgh/London
*It was (**very**) **much colder** in Edinburgh than in London.*

Cairo/Edinburgh
*It was **far hotter** in Cairo than in Edinburgh.*

1 Alexandria/Cairo
2 Glasgow/Edinburgh
3 Malaga/London
4 Helsinki/Stockholm
5 Riyadh/Alexandria
6 Cairo/Munich
7 Edinburgh/Moscow
8 Luxor/Alexandria
9 Barcelona/Madrid
10 Melbourne/Sydney

WORLD TEMPERATURES
Lunch time reports

	°C	°F		°C	°F
Alexandria	28	82	Madrid	27	80
Barcelona	25	77	Malaga	20	68
Cairo	30	86	Melbourne	16	60
Edinburgh	12	53	Moscow	12	53
Glasgow	14	57	Munich	30	86
Helsinki	13	55	Riyadh	39	102
Las Palmas	28	82	Stockholm	23	73
London	20	68	Sydney	23	73
Luxor	35	100	Tenerife	30	86

46 conditional: progressive conditional (BEU 88.1)

What would they be doing if . . . ?

▶ He's doing his homework.
If he wasn't doing his homework,
he**'d be playing** football. (1)

1 He's doing his homework.

2 He's teaching.

3 He's having a hard day at the office.

4 She's working late.

5 He's mending his car.

6 She's doing the housework.

7 He's practising the piano.

47 conditional: use (BEU 88.2a)

What would you do if. . . ?

▶ Suppose someone stole your car. . .
If someone stole my car I **would** *report it to the police immediately.*

1 Suppose you left a restaurant with the wrong umbrella. . .
2 Suppose a waiter in a restaurant overcharged you. . .
3 Suppose you missed the last bus home. . .
4 Suppose you missed your station on the train. . .
5 Suppose you got lost in a big city. . .

6 Suppose someone stole your wallet. . .
7 Suppose you lost your passport. . .
8 Suppose a stranger asked you for a lift at night. . .
9 Suppose someone offered you a briefcase full of money. . .
10 Suppose you got stuck in a lift. . .

48 conjunctions (BEU 89.3)

Say these things another way. Use *because, so, although, but, as, that*.

▶ Because I hadn't worked hard enough, I didn't pass the exam.
*I hadn't worked hard enough, **so** I didn't pass the exam.*

1 As we all know, English is a difficult language to learn well.
2 You can see that I'm very busy.
3 Although the sun's shining, it isn't very warm.
4 He's very rich, but he doesn't waste money.
5 I hadn't saved enough money, so I couldn't buy a car.
6 Because I liked him, I trusted him.
7 I didn't trust him, so I didn't help him.
8 As you will understand, I can't pay the whole sum at once.
9 She's very busy, but she's always willing to help.
10 Although he's very fat, he doesn't eat much.

49 'copula' verbs (BEU 91)

Describe these pictures with *look, sound, smell, taste* or *feel*, as in the example. Use *beautiful, bitter, burnt, delicious, delightful, expensive, hot, lonely, soft, cold, sad, happy, terrible.*

▶ They **look** happy. (1)

1

2

3

4

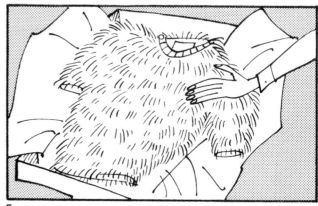

5

50   countable and uncountable nouns   (BEU 92)

Use *a/an* or no article, as necessary.

▶ *English people often have:*
  orange juice, cornflakes (or other cereal),
  porridge, boiled eggs, bacon (or ham) and eggs,
  toast or rolls with butter, jam or marmalade, tea or
  coffee.

Simon has:
a glass of orange juice, **a** boiled egg, **a** piece of
toast with butter and jam, two cups of tea.

1   What do people in your country often have for breakfast?
2   What do you usually have for breakfast?

51   dates   (BEU 95)

Can you match the horoscope
signs with the dates? Say the dates
aloud and write them in words
(either British English or American
English).

▶ *Aquarius, from January the*
  twenty-first to February the
  nineteenth. (British English)

21st January – 19th February
20th February – 20th March
21st March – 20th April
21st April – 21st May
22nd May – 21st June
22nd June – 23rd July
24th July – 23rd August
24th August – 23rd September
24th September – 23rd October
24th October – 22nd November
23rd November – 21st December
22nd December – 20th January

52   dates   (BEU 95.2)

When and where did the Olympic Games take place?
Say the date aloud and write it in words.

▶ *1960, Rome or Athens?*
  In 1960 (nineteen sixty), the Olympic Games were held in Rome.

1   1964, Tokyo or Madrid?
2   1968, Lisbon or Mexico City?
3   1972, Delhi or Munich?
4   1976, Montreal or Buenos Aires?
5   1980, Budapest or Moscow?
6   1984, London or Los Angeles?

53 **do**: auxiliary verb (BEU 98.1,2)

Which of these things don't you do?
Which of these things can't you do?

▶ I **don't** listen to jazz.
I **can't** write shorthand.

drink strong coffee	like snakes
stay out late at night	travel a lot
go to bed early	enjoy walking
smoke	ski
believe in horoscopes	like horror films
like music	listen to jazz
write shorthand	play the trumpet
speak Chinese	watch much television
drive a car	enjoy washing up

54 **do + -ing** (BEU 99)

Make 10 true sentences.

▶ I don't **do** much **cleaning** at the weekends.

I	do don't do	a lot of much some the my	shopping cleaning swimming etc	at the weekends in the evenings in winter etc.

55 **do** and **make** (BEU 100)

Continue the two columns, as in the example.

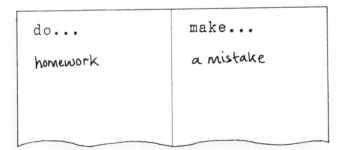

a mistake, homework, a favour, a journey, the beds, a cake, housework, bread, arrangements, a decision, business, the washing-up, an excuse, one's best, one's duty, the shopping, a model plane, a phone call, the cooking, military service

56 **during** and **for** (BEU 101)

during or *for*?

CAROL   I'm going to Mexico ___1___ two months this summer.

PAT   Oh, it's a fascinating country. I was there ___2___ the summer vacation last year, but only ___3___ a month. I'm going to India this year.

CAROL   I stayed in Calcutta ___4___ a while a few years ago. I met some very interesting people there ___5___ my stay. I went to Canada last year with two friends, on a peaceful fishing holiday. It was certainly peaceful – we didn't see anyone else ___6___ three weeks! ___7___ the day it was beautiful, but ___8___ the night we often heard strange noises and couldn't get to sleep ___9___ hours. In summer it's lovely and warm, but I wouldn't like to be there ___10___ the winter.

57 **during** and **in** (BEU 102)

during, in or both?

1 We went to the theatre last night, but I fell asleep _____ the performance.
2 We shall be out of the country _____ the whole of May and June.
3 John met Janet _____ his apprenticeship.
4 They met _____ August and got married _____ September.
5 Where was Polly _____ the concert?
6 There was nobody on the streets _____ the football match.
7 Do you sometimes wake up _____ the night?
8 I had a headache _____ the interview and didn't do very well.
9 'What happened to Lopez _____ the race?' 'He slipped and fell.'
10 Do you go out much _____ the week?

58 **each other** and **one another** (BEU 105)

What do good friends usually do? Make sentences with *each other/one another*.

▶ *Good friends tell **each other/one another** secrets.*
   *Good friends borrow **one another's** books or records.*
   *Good friends buy **each other** a meal or a drink.*

Continue . . .

59 **else** (BEU 109)

Put in one of the following + *else/else's*:

what	much	where
who	everybody	everything
nobody	nothing	everywhere
somebody	anything	

▶ I've looked everywhere. There's *nowhere else* to look.

1 We've asked everybody. There's _____ to ask.
2 I left the restaurant with _____ umbrella.
3 He works for a computer company and lives in London. I'm afraid I don't know _____ about him.
4 I don't know why Jim is against the suggestion. _____ welcomed it.
5 _____ did you go besides Peru and Chile?
6 I got lots of presents besides the watch. Let me show you _____ I got.
7 I'll look for the book in the bathroom now. I've already looked _____ .
8 Is there _____ you'd like to tell me? No, _____ at all.
9 It must have been Janet who told you that! _____ would say such a thing?
10 I don't like telling lies to my boss, but _____ can I do?

60 emphatic structures with **it** (BEU 111)

Rewrite the sentences in four different ways, beginning *It was . . . that . . .*, to emphasize different ideas.

▶ John drove Diana to the airport on Sunday .

   a *It was John **that** drove Diana to the airport on Sunday.*
   b *It was Diana **that** John drove to the airport on Sunday.*
   etc

1 John drove Diana to the airport on Sunday .
2 Jill phoned her mother from Paris last week .
3 Mrs Brown met Sally in the supermarket yesterday .

61 enjoy (BEU 112)

Which of these activities do you enjoy?
Which don't you enjoy?

▶ *I **enjoy** meeting people.*

---

62 enough (BEU 113.1)

Complete the sentences with a suitable adjective or
adverb + *enough*, as in the example.

▶ Janet wants to get married, but her parents are
against it. They don't think she is **old enough**.

1 I've never won anything in my life. I'm not
   _____ .

2 Tom tried to lift the heavy box, but he wasn't
   _____

3 I don't think Pam Morris will pass the examination.
   She doesn't work _____ .

4 Smith didn't win the race. He can't sprint _____ .

5 Don't dive into the water. It isn't _____ .

6 The child can't reach the light switch. He isn't
   _____

7 I couldn't hear what they were saying. They
   weren't speaking _____ .

8 We didn't go in the sea. It wasn't _____ .

9 Karlová didn't win the tennis match. She didn't
   play _____ .

10 I don't think Marion will ever become a good
   interpreter. She doesn't speak _____ .

63 enough (BEU 113.2)

Ted's going to have a party. He needs more food and drink etc. Look at his list. Say what he has got/hasn't got enough of.

▶ He's got **enough** orange juice.

	need	have got
orange juice	4 bottles	4 bottles
Coca Cola	4 bottles	1 bottle
beer	6 bottles	2 bottles
wine	2 bottles	2 bottles
sausage rolls	12	3
cheese biscuits	3 packets	1 packet
packets of crisps	4 packets	4 packets
chocolate biscuits	3 packets	4 packets
glasses	6	5
plates	6	6
chairs	6	2

64 enough (BEU 113.3)

In your country, is a young person of 16 old enough to do these things?

▶ vote?
*He/she isn't **old enough** to vote.*

1 vote?
2 ride a motor-bike?
3 leave school?
4 buy cigarettes?
5 drive a car?
6 open a bank account?
7 earn money?
8 live alone?
9 be sent to prison?
10 get married?

65 even though (BEU 114.4)

Rewrite with *Even though*, as in the example.

▶ Mary's very pretty, but she hasn't got a boyfriend.
Even though *Mary's very pretty, she hasn't got a boyfriend.*

1 I didn't work very hard for the exam, but I passed.
2 I don't speak Greek, but I made a lot of friends in Athens.
3 Mr Collins doesn't earn much, but he's always well dressed.
4 Sylvia hasn't got many friends, but she's always out.
5 Robert hasn't had a good education, but he's got a good job.
6 Jill Stewart has four children, but her house is always clean and tidy.
7 Mrs Poole doesn't eat much, but she puts on weight.
8 Terry has stopped smoking, but he still has a cough.
9 The sun didn't shine all day, but it was very warm.
10 I sat in the shade all day, but I got a sun-tan.

66 ever (BEU 116)

You would like to know more about a person who interests you. Ask him/her questions with *Have you ever . . . ? Do you ever . . . ?* Think of your own interests and the places you have been to.

▶ **Do you ever** *go to discos?*
Have you ever *been to America?*

67 **except** and **except for** (BEU 119)

Which one is different? Make sentences with *all* and
except, as in the example.

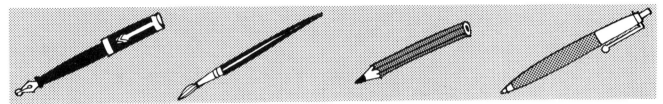

► *They're **all** used for writing (We write with them all/They all write) **except** the paintbrush.*
  or
  *They **all** have metal parts **except** the pencil.*

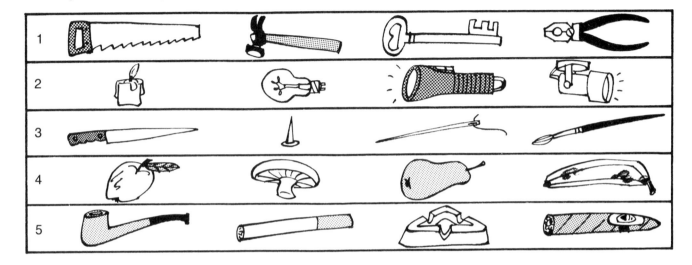

Now make sentences with *except for* and *all*, as in the example.

► ***Except for** the tyre, they are **all** completely round.*

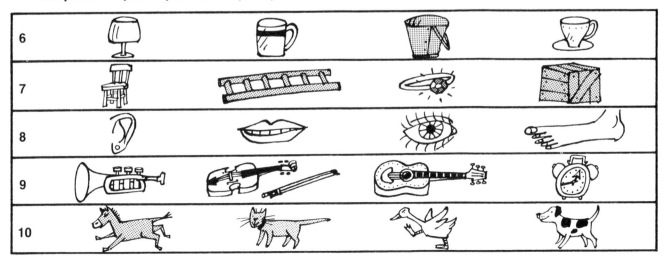

68 exclamations (BEU 120.1,2)

Make typical exclamations with *How . . . !* or *What . . . !*

▶ **How** expensive!
What a price!
What a lot of money! (1)

1

2

3

4

5

6

7

8

9

69 explain (BEU 123)

Match expressions from the two lists, and put them into sentences
with *explain(s) . . . to you*, as in the example.

▶ *A lawyer **explains** the law **to you**.*
*Teachers **explain** school subjects **to you**.*

A dictionary	the weather
A grammar	the law
Politicians	your illnesses
Teachers	the news
Scientists	school subjects
Meteorologists	human behaviour
A lawyer	the meanings of words
A doctor	language rules
A journalist	their policies
Religion	the natural world
A psychologist	the meaning of life

70 fairly, quite, rather and pretty (BEU 124)

Put in the correct word(s). In which sentences are both
words correct?

1 I _____ like Susan's boyfriend. He's nice.
(*quite/fairly*)

2 The film wasn't bad. We _____ liked it.
(*fairly/rather*)

3 I spent a year in Mexico, so my Spanish is
_____ good. (*pretty/rather*)

4 It was _____ a nice party. (*pretty/quite*)

5 My brother's a lawyer – a _____ successful one,
in fact. (*fairly/quite*)

6 Are you warm enough? I think it's _____ cold in
here. (*rather/pretty*)

7 I _____ enjoy driving on country roads. It's
relaxing. (*fairly/rather*)

8 'Are you a good cook?' 'A _____ good one, I
suppose.' (*quite/fairly*)

9 I met _____ an interesting man yesterday.
(*quite/rather*)

10 You speak Chinese _____ well, don't you? How
did you learn it? (*rather/pretty*)

71 far and a long way (BEU 125)

far or *a long way*?

MICHAEL   Where do you live?
JOANNE   In Green Street. Not very __1__ from here,
really. But it's quite __2__ on foot.
MICHAEL   Is it as __3__ as it is to Jerry's place?
JOANNE   No, not as __4__ as that. Jerry lives
__5__ from here, in the other direction.
MICHAEL   Well, get in and I'll drive you home. But
there isn't much petrol in the tank. How __6__ is it
to the nearest filling station?
JOANNE   Oh, it's __7__ from here, I'm afraid.
Certainly too __8__ to walk! How __9__ will the
petrol take us?
MICHAEL   I'm not sure, but __10__ enough, I hope.
We'll risk it.

72 farther and further (BEU 126)

farther, further or both?

1 Let's stop here. It's not safe to go any _____ .
2 These offices are closed until _____ notice.
3 If you have any _____ questions, please ask Mr Hill.
4 Which is _____ , the supermarket or the bank?
5 I can't walk any _____ , I'm too tired.
6 The police need _____ facts.
7 You will receive _____ training on the job.
8 The airport is _____ away than the station.
9 If you need _____ information, write to this address.
10 The machine is broken. It can't be put to _____ use.

73 (a) few and (a) little (BEU 129)

(a) few or *(a) little*?

Only __1__ people choose to live in the centre of a large town – most people have __2__ choice. They usually dream of a house in the country, where there are no traffic-jams and no industry, very __3__ noise and dirt, only __4__ cars and lorries, and __5__ pollution. But there are some disadvantages, too.

There are usually only __6__ jobs in the area, __7__ shops and restaurants close by, __8__ leisure-time facilities and __9__ opportunity of meeting people and making new friends.

What would you do, if you had the choice?

74 (a) few and (a) little (BEU 129)

You haven't been shopping for over a week. You haven't got much/many of the following things. What is there left? Use *a little* and *a few*.

▶ *There's **a little** cheese left, and there are **a few** eggs.*

75 fewer and less (BEU 130)

If you want to have a healthier diet, what should you eat *fewer*, *less* or *more* of?

▶ chocolate, biscuits, fresh fruit
  *You should eat **less** chocolate, **fewer** biscuits and **more** fresh fruit.*

1 salt, fried foods, fresh vegetables
2 raw salads, canned foods
3 sugar, sweet foods, honey
4 fish, meat, eggs
5 vegetable oils, butter
6 white bread, wholemeal bread
7 cream, natural yoghurt, puddings
8 coffee, caffeine-free drinks, cola-drinks
9 alcohol, fresh natural fruit juices
10 salted nuts, soya beans

76 **fewer** and **less** (BEU 130)

Compare today with 25 years ago. What were there fewer of? What was there less of?

▶ *There was **less** pollution.*
*There were **fewer** factories.*

Continue...

pollution	unemployment
factories	nuclear weapons
industry	danger of world war
crime	inflation
motorways	people out of work
road deaths	millionaires
traffic	terrorists

77 **for**: purpose (BEU 131.1)

Say what you would go to the following places for:

▶ a snack bar
*I'd go to a snack-bar **for** a quick meal or a sandwich.*

1 the post office
2 the library
3 the doctor's
4 the newsagent's
5 a restaurant

6 the bank
7 the baker's
8 the supermarket
9 the travel agent's
10 the chemist's

78 **for**: purpose (BEU 131.2)

What are these things called? What do we use them for?
Begin with *That's* ... or *Those are* ...

▶ 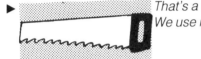 *That's a saw.*
*We use it **for sawing** wood.*

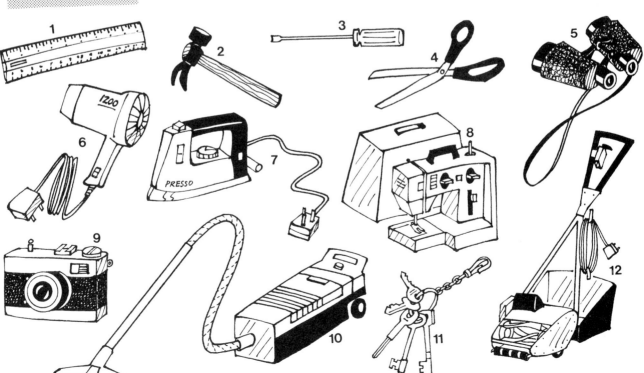

79 **for** + object + infinitive (BEU (132.1)

Answer these questions about your country as in the example.

> Do women go out to work? *(common/unusual)*
> *Yes, it's common **for women to go out to work**.*
> *No, it's unusual **for women to go out to work**.*

1 Do pupils attend school until they are 16 or older? *(usual/rare)*
2 Do people own a house or flat? *(common/rare)*
3 Do people have several children? *(normal/ uncommon)*
4 Do women usually have a driving licence? *(common/rare)*
5 Do old people live with their children? *(usual/ uncommon)*

6 Do women join the armed forces? *(common/rare)*
7 Do unmarried couples live together? *(common/ unusual)*
8 Do people usually join a political party or trade union? *(usual/rare)*
9 Are great numbers of people unemployed? *(common/rare)*
10 Do people learn English at school? *(normal/ unusual)*

---

80 **for** + object + infinitive (BEU 132.1)

Rewrite as in the example.

> ▶ People in Britain often fail their driving test the first time. *(It's normal…)*
> *It's normal **for people in Britain to fail** their driving test the first time.*

1 Learners often have to take their driving test three times. *(It's also quite common…)*
2 Most people pass the test the second time. *(It's usual…)*
3 All beginners should take some lessons with a driving instructor. *(It's important…)*
4 The driving instructor usually points out mistakes. *(It's usual…)*
5 Learner drivers should keep their eyes on the road, not on the signs. *(It's essential…)*

6 Nervous drivers should try to keep calm. *(It's important…)*
7 The learner should try to feel confident and not panic. *(It's quite essential…)*
8 Most people usually feel very nervous on the day of the test. *(It's quite normal…)*
9 Examiners are usually quite strict. *(It's usual…)*
10 A nervous driver doesn't usually pass the test the first time. *(It's rare…)*

---

81 **for** and **since** (BEU 133.1–3)

This is Bill

and this is Mary.

Here are some facts about them. Put in *for* (6 times) and *since* (4 times) with the date (year) or number of years, as in the example.

Bill was born in 1950. He met Mary when he was 20. Now he's 35, so he's known her *for 15 years*. They got married 12 years ago, when Bill was 23. Now it's 1985, so they've been married ___1___ . Bill started work when he was 18, so he had worked ___2___ before he got married. After they got married in 1973, Mary kept her job until 1979, so she worked ___3___ after their marriage. Then they had a child. Now he's 6. Bill has worked for his present firm for 10 years, ___4___ . He's an accountant. Before then, he worked for a smaller firm. He started there in 1971, so altogether he worked for them ___5___ . Bill and Mary bought a house 5 years ago, so they've had it ___6___ . They bought a new car 2 years ago, so they've had that ___7___ . Their last holiday was in 1982 – no money, so they haven't been on holiday ___8___ . Their little boy started school at the age of 5, so he's been going to school ___9___ . Three months later, Mary started a part-time job, so she's had the job ___10___ .

82 **for** and **since** (BEU 133.4)

How long have you been doing these things?
Answer with *for* or *since* the questions that apply to you.

▶ How long have you been learning English?
*I've been learning English **for three years**/**since 1982**.*

1 How long have you lived in your town?
2 How long have your parents lived in your town?
3 How long have you been living in your present house/flat?
4 How long have you been able to ride a bicycle/drive a car?

5 How long have you had a bicycle/car?
6 How long have you known your best friend?
7 How long have you known your English teacher?
8 How long have you been able to swim?
9 How long have you been engaged/married?
10 How long have you had your present job?

83 future: present progressive (BEU 135.1)

Say what you are doing (or what somebody else is doing) at the following times.

▶ after supper tonight?
*I'm **going straight to bed** after supper tonight.*

tomorrow evening?
*My sister's **going out** tomorrow evening.*

1 After supper tonight?
2 Tomorrow evening?
3 On Saturday?
4 On Sunday?
5 On your/his/her next holiday?

84 future: **going to** (BEU 135.2)

What's going to happen?

▶ *The car's **going to** overturn.* (1)

1
2

3
4
5
6

7
8
9
10

85 future: **going to** (BEU 135.2)

What are you going to do this evening? Are you going
to do any of the following things?

▶ I'm **going to watch** television.
    I'm not **going to wash** my hair.

86 future: **shall/will** (predictions)   (BEU 136)

What will life be like 100 years from now? Here are
some ideas:

▶ *There won't be any more cars. Most people will fly
private helicopters. Robots will do housework.
Computers will do office work. Children won't
have to go to school; they'll learn from computers
at home.*

Ideas

computers	leisure time
space travel	travel
traffic	air pollution
cars	supersonic planes
working conditions	population explosion
robots	

87 future: **shall/will** (predictions)   (BEU 136)

What questions would you ask a fortune-teller?
Begin with *Will . . .* and *What/When/How long/Where* etc.

▶ *Will I get married?*
What will my husband/wife be like?
Where will I live?

88 future: simple present   (BEU 138.1)

What are Jim's travel arrangements for his trip to the
International Book Fair in Frankfurt?
Use *depart, arrive, cross, stay, travel,* etc.

▶ *He **leaves** Doncaster by train at 16.10 and . . .*

```
dep. Doncaster 16.10
arr. London, Kings Cross 17.49
overnight in London, Victoria Hotel
dep. London, Victoria 8.00
arr. Dover 9.25
Jetfoil 10.00
arr. Ostend 11.40
dep. Ostend 12.15
arr. Frankfurt 19.10
```

89 future perfect   (BEU 139)

The table shows the most densely
populated cities/areas of the world
in millions, with approximate
estimates for the year 2000.

Compare the information as in
the examples:

▶ *By the year 2000, the
population of Mexico will have
increased from 15 million to
26.3 million.*

*By the year 2000, Mexico will
have moved up to first position.*

*By the year 2000, New York
will have gone down to
sixth position.*

	1980	m		**2000**	m
1	Tokyo	17.0	1	Mexico City	26.3
2	New York	15.6	2	São Paulo	24.0
3	Mexico City	13.0	3	Tokyo	17.1
4	São Paulo	12.8	4	Calcutta	16.6
5	Shanghai	11.8	5	Bombay	16.0
6	Buenos Aires	10.1	6	New York	15.5
7	London	10.0	7	Seoul	13.5
8	Calcutta	9.5	8	Shanghai	13.5
9	Los Angeles	9.5	9	Rio de Janeiro	13.3
10	Rhine-Ruhr (W. Germany)	9.3	10	Delhi	13.3
11	Rio de Janeiro	9.2	11	Buenos Aires	13.2
12	Beijing	9.1	12	Cairo	13.2

Write about Tokyo São Paulo Shanghai Buenos Aires Calcutta
Rio de Janeiro Bombay Seoul

90 future perfect (BEU 139)

How much will they have saved? Write sentences.

▶ *Terry will have saved £100 in 2 months' time.*

Terry	£50 a month
Janet	£8 a week
Ted	£65 a month
Maria	£100 a month
Barry	spends everything
Jeff	£6 a week
Helen	£70 a month
Celia	doesn't save
Betty	£10 a week
John	spends everything

1 Terry, in 3 months' time?
2 Janet, in 6 weeks' time?
3 Ted, in 4 months' time?
4 Maria, in 6 months' time?
5 Barry, in a month's time?
6 Jeff, in 10 weeks' time?
7 Helen, in 3 months' time?
8 Celia, in a month's time?
9 Betty, in 10 weeks' time?
10 John, in 10 weeks' time?

How much will you have saved six months from now?

91 future progressive (BEU 140)

Mr Green is flying to Paris tomorrow. Here's his notebook.

What will he be doing tomorrow at the following times?

▶ 6.20
At 6.20 tomorrow he'll be driving to the airport by taxi.

1	8.00	5	10.15	9	15.45
2	8.55	6	12.15	10	16.30
3	9.20	7	14.15	11	18.00
4	9.30	8	15.00	12	18.30

6.15 taxi to airport
7.30 flight leaves
8.55 arrival / Paris
9.20 meet M. Chevalier, drive to company headquarters
10.00 meeting with Board of Directors
12.00 lunch with Max Peters
14.00 lecture (don't forget lecture notes!)
15.00 phone New York !
15.30 meeting with Bill Morris (project CX12)
16.30 leave for airport
17.00 arrival at airport
18.00 flight home leaves
19.30 flight lands

92 get + noun/pronoun, adjective (BEU 142.1,2)

What does *get* mean in the following sentences?

1 The phone's ringing. I'll *get* it.
2 I was in the supermarket today, so I *got* you some of those cheap chocolate biscuits.
3 We couldn't go to London because Fred *got* flu.
4 I can't *get* the lid off the jar of jam.
5 What time did you *get* there?
6 Can you *get* Luxemburg on your transistor?
7 I'm sorry, but I didn't *get* the joke.
8 You didn't *get* the thief, but did you at least *get* the car number?
9 Hurry up and eat your breakfast, before it *gets* cold!
10 How did you *get* the piano through the door?
11 The shop had sold out of those new tin openers, but they're going to *get* me one.
12 I *got* a parcel from Aunt Susan this morning.

93 go: been and gone (BEU 145.1)

Where has he been? Write sentences saying
which cities/countries Mr Smith has been to.

▶ **He's been** to Athens/Greece. (1)

Which foreign countries have you been to?
Think of people you know who are abroad at the moment.
Say where they have *gone*.

▶ My father's **gone** to Mexico.

94 **go** meaning 'become' (BEU 146.2)

Use *bad*, *dry*, *flat*, *hard*, *stale*, *limp*, *soft*, or *sour* to say what happens, as in the example.

▶ What happens to fish if you leave it in the sun?
  It **goes** bad.

1 What happens to butter if you leave it where it's warm?
2 What happens to cheese if you don't wrap it?
3 What happens to sugar if it gets damp?
4 What happens to meat if you don't keep it cool?
5 What happens to chocolate if you leave it in the sun?
6 What happens to lemonade if you don't put the top on the bottle?
7 What happens to milk if you leave it in the sun?
8 What happens to bread if you don't wrap it?
9 What happens to lettuce if you don't cool it?

95 **go . . . -ing** (BEU 147)

Do you ever do any of the following sports? Use *sometimes*, *never*, etc and *go . . . + ing*.

▶ I **never** go cross-country skiing. (1)

1

2

3

4

5

6

7

8

9

10

11

12

13

14

96 **had better** (BEU 148)

Draw conclusions and give advice using *had better*.

▶ Your hands are dirty.
   *You'**d better** wash them.*

1 You look very tired.
2 Your hair's too long.
3 You've lost a button from your coat.
4 You'll be late for work.
5 The milk tastes sour.

6 The toast is burnt.
7 You have a temperature.
8 This medicine will make you better.
9 Your car's dirty.
10 That letter's important.

---

97 **hard** and **hardly** (BEU 150)

hard or *hardly*?

1 It was dark, so we could _____ see.
2 If you want to score a goal, kick the ball _____ !
3 John has _____ said a word all day.
4 I went to the meeting, but _____ anybody was there.
5 You'll have to work _____ if you want to pass the examination.
6 You have to practise _____ if you want to play the piano well.

7 You _____ ever practise, do you?
8 Julia has been working _____ all day.
9 Terry's an excellent student. He gets _____ anything wrong!
10 I'm not much good at tennis. I don't hit the ball _____ enough.

---

98 **have**: possession etc (BEU 153.1)

Which countries have a king, a queen, an emperor or a sultan?

▶ The United Kingdom
   *The United Kingdom **has** a queen.*

1 Thailand?
2 Japan?
3 Norway and Sweden?
4 Oman?
5 Denmark and Holland?

6 Belgium?
7 Morocco?
8 Brunei?
9 Spain?
10 Saudi Arabia and Jordan?

99 **have (got)**: possession etc (BEU 153.2)

Have you or your family got any of these?

▶ I**'ve got** a tent.
We **haven't got** a piano.
My brother**'s got** a bicycle.

100 **have**: actions (BEU 154)

Say what Frank and Janet do and
when they do it. Use *have*.

► Before breakfast
Frank **has a shower**
before breakfast.

Before breakfast

At 8 o'clock

At 10 o'clock

At 12.30

After lunch

At 3 o'clock

After work

In the evening: sometimes

In the evening: usually

At the weekend: often

At the weekend: sometimes

101 **have** + object + past participle (BEU 155.2)

What are they having done?

▶ *She's **having her**
  hair done.* (1)

102 **have** + object + past participle (BEU 155.2)

Have you ever had any of these things done?

▶ your eyes tested?
*No, I've never **had my eyes tested**.*
*Yes, I've **had my eyes tested** twice/several times.*

1 a tooth extracted?
2 your heart examined?
3 your hearing tested?
4 your blood pressure checked?
5 a blood sample taken?
6 your lungs X-rayed?

103 **have (got) to** (BEU 156)

What have you got to do? Write ten sentences about things that you've got to do next week.

▶ *On Monday, I**'ve got to go** to the dentist's.*

104 **have (got) to** (BEU 156)

What do you think are the disadvantages of these jobs?
Use *you have to . . .*

▶ air hostess
*You **have to travel** most of the time. You **have to work** irregular hours. You **have to deal with** difficult passengers.*

1 businessman
2 coal miner
3 factory worker
4 football player
5 hairdresser
6 photographic model
7 office worker
8 postman
9 shop assistant
10 waitress

105 **hear** and **listen (to)** (BEU 157)

Put in a form of *hear, listen* or *listen to.*

POLICEMAN Now, what exactly did you __1__ on the night of the murder?
MRS GREEN Well, I could __2__ loud voices next door – a man and a woman, but I was busy in the kitchen, so I wasn't really __3__ what they were saying. But then I __4__ a loud bang! So I stopped what I was doing to __5__ .
POLICEMAN What was your husband doing at the time?
MRS GREEN Well, he was __6__ a music programme on the radio. I told him to turn it down so that I could __7__ better. But he's rather deaf, so he didn't __8__ me. And he never really __9__ what I say, in any case. But then the shouting started. I put my ear to the wall and __10__ as well as I could. I

__11__ the man say quite clearly: 'You'll never cheat me again!' And then the shots! I couldn't believe it!
POLICEMAN Did your husband __12__ the shots as well?
MRS GREEN No, the music was too loud, and he says he wasn't __13__ anyway.

106 home (BEU 161)

Complete with a suitable verb + *home*. Use each verb once: *arrive, bring, come, drive, get, go, leave, reach, run, take, walk*.

▶ *We left early in the morning, but we didn't **reach home** until late evening.*

1 We _____ at 8 am and arrived in Edinburgh at 4 pm.
2 It's very late. I really must _____ now.
3 Goodbye! Have a good time and don't _____ late!
4 If you leave now, you should _____ at about 6 o'clock.
5 We'll pack for the weekend, but if we don't find a hotel room, we'll simply _____ .

6 My wife's picking blackberries in the woods. Last Sunday she _____ nearly four pounds.
7 What time did you _____ last night?
8 There was a thunderstorm on the way, so we _____ as fast as we could.
9 I missed the last bus, so I had to _____ .
10 Bill doesn't earn much money. He says he _____ only a hundred pounds a week.

---

107 if: ordinary tenses (BEU 164.1)

What happens if . . . ? Complete the sentences.

▶ If you don't get enough sleep, *you always feel tired.*
  If you sit in the hot sun for too long, you get sunburnt.

1 If you stand in the cold for a long time, _____ .
2 If you run uphill, _____ .
3 If you drink too much alcohol, _____ .
4 If you get caught in the rain without an umbrella, _____ .
5 If you don't have a job, _____ .

6 _____ , you put on weight.
7 _____ , you lose weight.
8 _____ , your eyes get tired.
9 _____ , you get a smoker's cough.
10 _____ , you get tooth decay.

---

108 if: special tenses (BEU 165.1)

What would you do/buy etc if you won the following amounts of money in your own currency?

1 £10
2 £100
3 £1,000
4 £10,000
5 £100,000
6 £1,000,000

109 **if**: special tenses, present and future situations   (BEU 165.1)

If you hired the following models,
how much would it cost?

▶ a Vauxhall Astra for 3 days?
*If you **hired** a Vauxhall Astra for
3 days it **would cost** £66.00.*

1 a Ford Sierra for a weekend?
2 a BL Metro for 3 days?
3 a BMW 316 for 2 weeks?
4 a Ford Fiesta for 5 days?
5 a BL Montego for a week?
6 a Ford Orion for 2 weeks?
7 a Vauxhall Nova for a weekend?
8 a Ford Escort for 4 days?
9 a BL Maestro for 2 weeks?
10 a Vauxhall Cavalier for 3 weeks?

Hertz ®

LONDON BUDGET RATES
Pre-discounted rate. Must be pre-booked

GROUP	SEATS	Specific car models cannot be guaranteed MANUAL TRANSMISSION	SUNROOF	POWER STEERING	CASSETTE	RADIO	CARS MUST BE RETURNED TO RENTING BRANCH		
							DAILY UNLIMITED	WEEKLY UNLIMITED	WEEKEND ★ Fri 13·00hrs Mon 10·00hrs UNLIMITED
A	4	**FORD** Fiesta VAUXHALL Nova BL Metro				• • •	£20·50	£108·50	£42·00
B	4	**FORD** Escort 1.3L VAUXHALL Astra 1.3L BL Maestro 1.3L		•		• •	£22·00	£119·00	£47·00
C	5	**FORD** Sierra 1.6L **FORD** Orion 1.6L VAUXHALL Cavalier 1.6L BL Montego 1.6L		• • • •	• • •	• • •	£25·50	£140·00	£53·00
D	4	BMW 316	•	•	•	•	£38·50	£199·00	£85·00

---

110 **if**: special tenses, past situations   (BEU 165.3)

You have a friend who is careless with his/her things.
Say what would/wouldn't have happened if he/she had/hadn't done the following:

▶ He left his suitcase unattended at an airport. It got stolen.
*If he **hadn't left** his suitcase unattended, it **wouldn't have got** stolen.*

1 She forgot to lock the car. Her camera got stolen.
2 He left his wallet in a restaurant. It disappeared.
3 She left her watch lying about. It got broken.
4 He didn't lock the door of his flat. Thieves broke in.
5 She knocked her glasses off the table. They broke.
6 She didn't put her name on her suitcase. Someone took it by mistake.

7 He parked his car without lights. Another car ran into it.
8 He didn't look after his bicycle. It went rusty.
9 She left her parcels on a bus. Someone took them.
10 He didn't keep his passport in a safe place. It got lost.

---

111 **if**: special tenses, past situations   (BEU 165.3)

Jim's holiday to Tangier cost more than necessary. It would have cost less if he had done some things differently.

Jim flew from Manchester in June and stayed at the Casino Park Hotel. He booked a single room with full board and a view of the sea.

▶ *It **would have cost** less if he **hadn't booked** a room with a view of the sea.*

Continue. . .

From Gatwick to Tangier:

SUN TRAVEL

	Palace	Casino Park	
Departure May	£185	£210	(7 nights)
Departure June	£220	£245	

From Manchester: + £40

Extra charges (per person per night)
Full board £3   Single room £2
Room with view of the sea £1.50

112 if-sentences with **could** (BEU 166)

Your friend can't decide where to go on holiday. Make some suggestions about where he/she could go and what he/she could do. (He/She could visit famous buildings; practise languages; eat national dishes; do/ watch certain sports.)

▶ Spain
   *If you went to Spain, you **could** eat paella, lie in the sun, watch a bull-fight and speak Spanish.*

1	London	6	India
2	Scotland	7	Mexico
3	New York	8	Egypt
4	Paris	9	Switzerland
5	Kenya	10	Italy

113 if only (BEU 167)

Molly, Patsy, Richard and Frank all have regrets.

▶ Molly can't swim very well.
   *She often thinks to herself, '**If only** I **could** swim well.*

   Richard broke off his engagement.
   *He often thinks to himself, '**If only** I **hadn't broken** off my engagement.'*

1 Patsy can't speak a foreign language.
2 Frank sold his old car.
3 Molly is afraid of water.
4 Richard failed his driving test.
5 Frank didn't take A-Level English at school.
6 Patsy left school at 16.
7 Molly can't play a musical instrument.
8 Richard didn't go to America when he had the chance.
9 Frank doesn't play tennis.
10 Richard isn't a good businessman.

114 imperative (BEU 170)

What advice would you give a friend who is going for a job interview? Here are some suggestions:

▶ ***Go to bed** early the night before.*
   ***Don't be** nervous.*
   ***Don't wear** your old jeans!*
   ***Have** a good breakfast – and **eat** it all.*

Continue . . .

115 imperative (BEU 170.1)

The Green Cross code tells you how to cross a road safely. Put in: *cross, find, give, keep, let, listen, look* (2), *move, remember, run, stand* (2), *stop, try, walk* (2). Be careful, some need *don't*!

1 First, _____ a safe place to cross, then _____ . _____ to cross between parked cars. _____ to a clear space and always _____ drivers a chance to see you clearly.
2 _____ on the pavement near the kerb. _____ too near the edge of the pavement.
3 _____ all around for traffic and _____ . You can sometimes hear traffic before you can see it.
4 If traffic is coming, _____ it pass. _____ all round again.

5 When there is no traffic, _____ straight across the road.
   If there is something in the distance, _____ unless you are certain there's plenty of time.
   _____ , even if traffic is a long way away, it may be coming very fast. When it's safe, _____ straight across – _____ !
6 _____ looking and listening for traffic while you cross.

116 imperative: with **do** (BEU 170.1)

Do you own a dog? The Dog Owners' Code tells you
how to look after a dog properly.
Complete it with *do* or *don't* + a suitable verb. Use
exercise, *feed*, *have*, *keep* (3), *leave*, *let* (3), *see*.

▶ *Do keep* him well under control in the country.

1 _____ him regularly. He needs a good run where it's safe.
2 _____ him run loose on the road.
3 _____ him clean – frequent brushing is the best way.
4 _____ him in a car with all the windows closed.
5 _____ that he has a dry place to sleep.
6 _____ children tease him.

7 _____ him regularly – one or two good meals every day at the same time. He needs fresh water too.
8 _____ him tied up or shut up for long periods.
9 _____ your name and address marked on his collar in case he gets lost.
10 _____ him foul pavements or grass areas.

117 in case (BEU 172.1,2)

Some friends are going on a day's hike. Tell them what
to take with them, just in case certain things happen.

▶ Take sleeping bags, **in case** you don't get home tonight.

1 Take warm pullovers _____ .
2 Take plenty to drink _____ .
3 Take enough food _____ .
4 Take waterproof clothing

_____ .
5 Take a map _____ .
6 Take a compass _____ .

7 Take your sunglasses

_____ .
8 Take some sticking plasters

_____ .
9 Take some money _____ .
10 Take some kind of identification _____ .

118 in spite of (BEU 173)

You have a friend who's very headstrong and does
things in spite of advice and warnings. Rewrite the
sentences, with *in spite of* + noun.

▶ He bought an old car, although it was in a bad condition.
*He bought an old car **in spite of** its bad condition.*

1 He drove the car 200 kilometres, although the roads were icy.
2 He drove the car up narrow mountain roads, although it was dangerous.
3 He tried to repair the car himself, although he was inexperienced as a mechanic.
4 He drove the car at night, although it was foggy.
5 He went sailing in his boat, although the weather forecast was bad.
6 He walked 10 kilometres, although it was snowing heavily.
7 He went out in the cold, although he was ill.

8 He smoked forty cigarettes a day, although his doctor warned him to stop smoking.
9 He bought an old house, although the price was high.
10 He married a girl who didn't suit him, although I advised him not to.

119 infinitive: verb + object + infinitive (BEU 176.3)

What do these advertisements want people to do?

▶ *Number one **wants people to book** a cruise.*
*Number two **wants you to invest** money.*

Continue. . .

20 infinitive: verb + object + infinitive (BEU 176.3)

Have you ever been swimming in Hawaii? If not, here's a warning to newcomers.

BEACH SAFETY

Hawaii's beaches are breathtakingly beautiful, but they can be very dangerous for newcomers. The beaches are always open, even when there is no lifeguard protection. If you do not see a lifeguard on duty, swim on another beach. Remember:

- Never turn your back on the ocean.
- Enter the water slowly and carefully.
- Don't be caught off your guard.
- Never swim alone.
- Always have someone you can call to.
- Dive beneath breaking waves before they reach you.
- Do not stand in the path of a large wave.
- Do not swim over a large wave or turn your back against it.
- Avoid beaches with rocky coasts.
- Stay clear of areas with surfers.
- Look out for runaway surfboards that wash in with the waves.

What does the warning *advise/remind/tell/warn* you to do or not to do?

► *It **advises** you to swim on another beach if you don't see a lifeguard on duty.*
*It **warns** you never to turn your back on the ocean.*

Continue...

---

121 infinitive after **who**, **what**, **how** etc (BEU 177.1)

A group of young Americans has come to stay in your town/area. What would you tell them/show them?
In your answers, use *who/when/where/what/whether/ how + (not) to*.

► *I would tell them **where to eat**.*
*I would show them **how to use** the buses.*

Ideas:	
hotels	shopping
transport	culture
sightseeing	money
entertainment	clothing
museums	information centres

122 infinitive of purpose (BEU 178)

Why would you go there?
Answer with *to*. . .

▶ *I'd go to a travel agency **to book** a holiday.* (1)

1

2

3

4

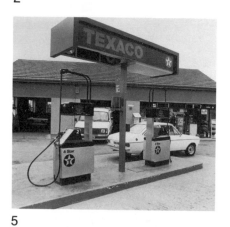

5

6

7

8

9

10

11

123 infinitive of purpose (BEU 178)

Why do some people need or use these things?

▶ sleeping pills
*Some people need sleeping pills **to help** them to sleep.*

1	an alarm clock	6	make-up
2	a walking stick	7	perfume/aftershave
3	glasses	8	artificial sweeteners
4	a hearing aid	9	medicine and tablets
5	hair dye	10	a safe

124 infinitive of purpose (BEU 178)

People all over the world learn English at evening classes or in special courses.
Why do you think the following groups of people need/want to learn English?
Use *in order to/so as to...*

▶ Hotel receptionists
*Hotel receptionists need English **in order to** talk to foreign guests.*

1	businessmen and -women	5	pilots
2	secretaries	6	housewives
3	scientists	7	journalists
4	engineers	8	people in the travel business

125 -ing form ('gerund') (BEU 180.2)

What are your hobbies? Name six things that you enjoy.

▶ *taking photographs, driving, listening to music,
playing chess, swimming, cooking.*

126 -ing form ('gerund') after verb: (BEU 180.3)

Study these activities:

going shopping wasting time
standing in crowded sunbathing
buses cooking
chatting on the telephone sewing on buttons
borrowing money arguing about money
looking after children making new friends
making excuses waiting at the doctor's
getting up early doing examinations
watching horror films sleeping late
writing thank-you letters smoking
taking on responsibility repairing things

Name all the things that...

▶ ... you usually try to avoid
*I usually try to avoid **standing** in crowded buses.*

1 ... you usually try to avoid.
2 ... you dislike.
3 ... you enjoy.
4 ... you often feel like.
5 ... you would like to give up.
6 ... you don't mind.
7 ... you often try to put off.
8 ... you don't like to risk.
9 ... you can't stand.

127 -ing form ('gerund') after **need** and **want** (BEU 180.4)

What needs doing?

▶   *The bed **needs making**.*

128 -ing form ('gerund') after preposition (BEU 180.5)

How can you become a millionaire?
Think of as many quick ways as possible, using
by . . . ing, as in the example.

▶   ***By making** a successful pop record.*
***By robbing** a bank!*

129 -ing form or infinitive? (BEU 182.1)

A friend of yours is going on holiday. Remind him of the things he must do.

▶ lock the door
Remember to/Don't forget to lock the door.

1 close the windows
2 cancel the newspapers
3 turn off the water and electricity
4 give your holiday address to the neighbours
5 ask the post office to forward your mail

On the plane, your friend thought about your advice. But he couldn't remember doing any of those things.

▶ He couldn't remember **locking** the door.

Continue. . .

130 irregular verbs (BEU 186)

Fill in the missing parts of these verbs.

Infinitive	Simple Past	Past Participle
awake		
		become
	broke	
bring		
catch		
		chosen
		fallen
	felt	
grow		
	kept	
know		
	laid	
	left	
		lain
	rode	
		risen
	shone	
		spent
steal		
	taught	
		worn

131 it's time (BEU 189.2)

Tell someone you know very well that it's time he/she did certain things.

▶ Your hair's greasy. **It's time** you washed it.

1 Your hair's too long.
2 You're too fat.
3 Your finger-nails are long.
4 Your shoes are dirty.
5 Your shirt's grubby.

6 Your socks smell.
7 Your room's untidy.
8 Your car's going rusty.
9 You owe me some money.
10 You've still got my dictionary.

132 let's (BEU 191)

What suggestions might you make
if you saw these?

▶ **Let's** have an ice-cream. (1)

1

2

3

4

5

6

7

8

9

10

11

133 look (at), watch and see (BEU 196)

look, look at, watch or *see*? Put in the correct form and tense.

1 My friend has _____ all the James Bond films.
2 How often do you _____ television?
3 I can _____ something strange in the sky.
4 We're going to _____ 'Hamlet' at the New Theatre tonight.
5 I _____ the paintings, but none of them was worth buying.
6 She sits for hours and _____ the birds in the garden.

7 If you _____ to the right, you'll see St. James's Palace.
8 I _____ an accident on my way here. Luckily, nobody was hurt.
9 Children, _____ the blackboard, please!
10 I've got a feeling that we are being _____ . Don't _____ round now. . . .

134 may and might: probability (BEU 199)

Write about some things that you *may* do during the next twelve months.

▶ I **may** go to the USA.
I **may** change my job.

135 may and might: possibility (BEU 199)

People often worry about things that *might* or *might not* happen.

▶ Sam's starting a new job next month.
*He's worried that he **might not** like it.*

1 Jean's going for an important job interview next week.
2 Mr Carter has heard that his factory is going to lay off 250 men.
3 Pamela's going to have her hair cut short.
4 My brother's earning less money than he used to. His car is becoming a luxury.
5 Cynthia Williams is taking an important examination tomorrow.

6 Sam's got a new boss. He doesn't like her.
7 Sally's boyfriend seems very interested in another girl.
8 Mrs Redstone has to finish a long report for her boss by Friday.
9 Jim has been promised a rise of 10 per cent, but he hasn't got it yet.
10 Robert's had a quarrel with his girlfriend.

136 may: permission (BEU 200.1)

You are a guest at someone's house for the first time. You don't know them very well and want to be particularly polite. Ask for what you want with *may*.

▶ You'd like to have another cup of tea.
May I have another cup of tea, please?

1 You'd like to use their telephone.
2 You'd like to smoke.
3 You want to write a letter, so you need some writing paper and an envelope.
4 It's rather cool in your room and you'd like to turn on the heating.
5 You'd like to have a shower.

6 There are some records in your room. You'd like to play them.
7 You can't reach the salt at table.
8 You'd like to look at the newspapers.
9 You'd like to watch the news on TV.
10 You'd like to have a walk round the garden.

137 **much**, **many**, **a lot** etc (BEU 205.1)

Do you eat or drink these things? How much?
Use *a lot of/lots of*, *many* or *much*.

▶ I eat **a lot of/lots of** vegetables.
 I don't eat **many** vegetables.
 I eat **a lot of** fish.
 I don't eat **much** fish.

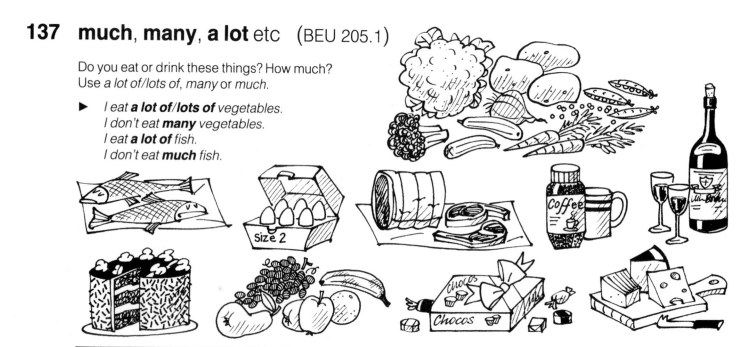

138 **must**: obligation (BEU 208)

I must...

▶ I've got an awful headache.
 *I **must** take an aspirin.*

Continue...

1 My watch is broken.
2 My car's very dirty.
3 I've got a terrible cold
 and a cough.
4 I'm getting too fat.
5 I've got an awful toothache.

6 I smoke too many cigarettes.
7 I've got a pile of unpaid bills.
8 I've written three
 important letters.
9 My hair's too long.
10 The kitchen's in a mess.

139 **must**: obligation (BEU 208)

In national parks all over the world, you will find signs
similar to these. What mustn't you do?

▶ *You **mustn't** pick the flowers.*

  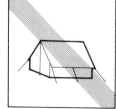  

40 **must**: deduction (BEU 210.1,2)

Who can they belong to?

▶ Who can the pipe belong to?
It can't belong to Liz or the children. It **must** *belong to Jim or Henry.*

141 **must**: deduction (BEU 210.3)

Use *must/can/can't have* to complete, as in the example.

▶ John said he would lend me his dictionary, but he hasn't given me it yet. *(He...)*
   He **must have** forgotten about it.

1 Where's Ted's old blue car? There's a lovely new red one parked in his garage! *(He...)*
2 I've rung Jill three times, but she didn't answer the phone. *(She...)*
3 Where has Joan put the box of chocolates? There must be some left. *(She...)*
4 Where are Bill's gloves? He can't find them anywhere. *(He...)*
5 I thought it was our secret, but Jane's mother knows all about it as well. *(Jane...)*

6 Terry's expecting me, but he hasn't answered the door. I'll ring again. *(He...)*
7 There's a young man lying at the side of the road and lots of people looking on. *(There...)*
8 I'm looking for Mary's keys. She left them in the kitchen. *(Where...)*
9 Where is Jack's wallet? He never took it out of his pocket, but it isn't there now. *(Someone...)*
10 Mark said he would ring as soon as he got home, but he hasn't done. *(He...)*

142 nationality words (BEU 212)

Which countries are these postage stamps from?

143 nationality words (BEU 212)

Which languages are spoken in these countries?

1 Argentina
2 Australia
3 Austria
4 Belgium
5 Brazil
6 Canada
7 Denmark
8 Holland
9 Egypt
10 Greece
11 Japan
12 Monaco
13 Switzerland
14 Thailand
15 Turkey
16 Wales

What is your native language?
What other languages do you speak or understand?

144 nationality words (BEU 212)

What nationality are they?
Begin *He's/She's a . . .*

▶ *He's a **Frenchman**.* (1)

1 François Mitterrand

2 Sophia Loren

3 Larry Hagman

4 Nana Mouskouri

5 Mikhail Gorbachev

6 Jane Fonda

7 Deng Xiaoping

8 Helmut Schmidt

9 Pope John Paul II

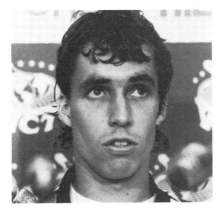

10 Ivan Lendl

11 Princess Diana

145 nationality words (BEU 212)

Say what the people from some of these countries are famous for.

▶ The **Austrians** are famous for their music.
The **French** make good wine.

Countries		
Austria	Greece	Russia
China	Holland	Scotland
France	Italy	Switzerland
Germany	Japan	Thailand
the USA		*Thais*

Ideas		
beer	cognac	silk
cameras	dancing	vodka
cars	food	watches
cheese	music	whisky
chocolate	perfume	wine

146 nationality words (BEU 212)

Can you match the country and the currency?
Use adjectives.

▶ The **Austrian** schilling, the **Brazilian** cruzeiro, . . .

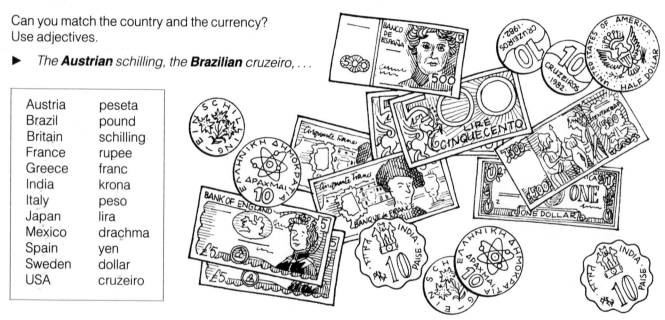

Austria	peseta
Brazil	pound
Britain	schilling
France	rupee
Greece	franc
India	krona
Italy	peso
Japan	lira
Mexico	drachma
Spain	yen
Sweden	dollar
USA	cruzeiro

147 need (BEU 213)

Put in *need, needn't, don't need, didn't need, needn't have* or *do . . . need.*

1 You _____ worry about me. Everything's going to be fine.
2 I _____ worked so hard for the exam. It was much easier than I expected.
3 The flowers _____ some water. They're very dry.
4 _____ *(we)* to book a table at the restaurant, or are there usually enough places free?
5 You _____ bother to see me to the door, thanks. I know the way.
6 I _____ bought so much wine. Everybody drank beer!

7 You _____ tell me if it's a secret. I understand.
8 We _____ to check the figures again. I don't think they're right.
9 We _____ set off too early. The train doesn't leave until 9.30.
10 I met Mary by chance in town, so I _____ to ring her yesterday.
11 You _____ repair the toaster. I'll do it myself.
12 The window-cleaner came earlier than usual, so I _____ to clean them myself.

148 neither (BEU 217.1)

Compare the hotels, using *neither*.

▶ The Bridge Hotel hasn't got rooms with a private bath.
  Neither has the Woodland Hotel.

1 The Bridge Hotel isn't a 2-star.
2 The Bridge Hotel hasn't got rooms with television.
3 The Crown Hotel doesn't give reduced rates for children.
4 The Bridge Hotel isn't open all the year round.
5 The Riverside Hotel hasn't got a bar.
6 The Crown Hotel doesn't offer free parking.
7 The Woodland Hotel hasn't got rooms with a private bath.
8 The Woodland Hotel hasn't got rooms with a telephone.
9 The Bridge Hotel hasn't got a lift.
10 The Woodland Hotel doesn't offer full board.

	Bridge Hotel	Crown Hotel	Riverside Hotel	Woodland Hotel
Cat.	★	★★	★★	★
🛁	–	15	12	–
CH	+	+	+	+
TV	–	+	+	–
☎	–	+	+	–
L	–	+	–	–
🍸	–	+	–	–
FB	–	+	+	–
– %	+	–	–	+
P	–	–	–	+
O	–	+	–	–

Cat. = category   🍸 = bar
🛁 = bathroom   FB = full board
CH = central heating   – % = reduced rates for children
TV = television
☎ = telephone   P = free parking
L = lift   O = open all year

149 neither...nor... (BEU 218)

Who didn't go where? A group of foreign students went to London, but unfortunately they didn't have enough time to see everything. Make sentences with *Neither...nor*.

▶ **Neither** Ali **nor** Pablos went to Madame Tussaud's.

Continue...

Places to see	Tick the places you saw						
	Ali	Elena	Pablos	José	Kirsten	Pierre	Yasuko
Oxford Street	√		√	√	√		√
10 Downing Street	√	√		√		√	√
Westminster Abbey	√	√	√		√		√
St Paul's Cathedral	√		√	√		√	√
Houses of Parliament		√		√	√	√	√
The British Museum		√	√		√	√	√
The Tower of London	√	√	√	√	√		
The Tate Gallery	√		√		√	√	√
A pub	√	√	√	√		√	
Madame Tussaud's		√		√	√	√	√
Speaker's Corner	√	√	√		√		√

150 next and nearest (BEU 219)

next or *nearest*?

1 Excuse me, when's the _____ train to Dover, please?
2 I always shop at Savewell's supermarket – simply because it's the _____ .
3 The _____ bank is in the _____ street on the right.
4 'Which bus stop is the _____ to the hospital, please?' 'Duke Street. We're almost there. It's the _____ stop.'
5 'Where's the _____ phone-box, please?' 'There's one just round the corner. If it's not working, the _____ one's just across the park.'

6 Who sits _____ to you in class?
7 This post-box has already been emptied. Let's try the _____ one.
8 'What do you do in an emergency?' 'You get the patient to the _____ doctor.'
9 'Where's Station Road, please?' 'Keep straight on, then turn right at the _____ traffic lights.'

customer
client
patient

151 no and none (BEU 221)

no, none or *neither*?

1 _____ of us is perfect.
2 I have two brothers, but _____ of them lives here.
3 _____ child is good all the time.
4 'How many of the answers did you get right?' '_____ !'
5 The question was difficult. _____ of the pupils knew the answer.

6 I rang him yesterday, but there was _____ reply.
7 Unfortunately, there was _____ time left for questions.
8 _____ of my parents had a good education.
9 _____ kind of drug is harmless – however mild.
10 'Can you come to the theatre with us tonight?' 'Sorry! _____ time, _____ money!'

152 no and not (BEU 222)

no or *not*?

1 I could come on Saturday, but _____ on Sunday.
2 'What's the time, please?' 'Sorry, I've got _____ idea.'
3 _____ smoking in the bus, please, sir!
4 'Is that the truth?' 'Well, no, _____ exactly.'
5 _____ book can give you an answer to *that* question!

6 _____ talking during the examination, please!
7 It was margarine that you bought, _____ butter.
8 _____ surprisingly, he failed the examination.
9 _____ men were there. Only women.
10 There was _____ coffee, so I made tea.

153 numbers (BEU 227.1)

Say the answers aloud and write them in words.

▶ $\frac{4}{5} - \frac{7}{10} = \frac{1}{10}$ (one tenth)

a $\frac{3}{5} + \frac{1}{10} = ?$

b $\frac{2}{3} - \frac{1}{2} = ?$

c $\frac{3}{4} - \frac{1}{8} = ?$

d $\frac{1}{8} + \frac{1}{4} + \frac{3}{8} = ?$

e $\frac{1}{3} + \frac{5}{6} - \frac{1}{2} = ?$

f $\frac{4}{5} + \frac{3}{10} - \frac{1}{2} = ?$

154 numbers (BEU 227.4)

Here are the numbers of some useful telephone services in England:

Operator Service	dial 100
Emergency	999
Inland Director Enquiry Operator	192
Traveline	
Road, Rail, Sea and Air information	
Rail (InterCity and London Services)	01-246 8030
Road (Motorways and major roads)	01-246 8031
Sea	01-246 8032
Air	01-246 8033
Travel conditions within 70 miles of London	01-246 8021
Leisureline	
Main Daily Events in London	
In English	01-246 8041
In French	01-246 8043
In German	01-246 8045
Weatherline	
Local weather conditions	
In London Area	01-246 8091
South Kent and Sussex Coast	01-246 8097
Timeline	
In London	dial 123
Sportsline	
Up to date information on major sporting events	01-246 8020

Say aloud the number you would dial if . . .

1 . . . you wanted to know the exact time.
2 . . . you wanted to hear what's on in London in French.
3 . . . you needed an ambulance urgently.
4 . . . you needed an inland telephone number.
5 . . . you wanted to hear the weather report for London.
6 . . . you wanted to hear the Wimbledon tennis results.
7 . . . you needed to send a Telemessage through the operator.
8 . . . you wanted to hear the London theatre programmes in English.
9 . . . you needed InterCity train services.
10 . . . you wanted to know whether any airports are closed.

155 numbers (BEU 227.5)

Choose your answers from the list and say them aloud.

Elizabeth I, Elizabeth II, Charles I, Charles III, Henry VIII, George VI.

1 Who became Queen of England in 1952?
2 Who was her father?
3 When Prince Charles becomes king, what will his title be?
4 Which queen ruled England from 1558 to 1603?
5 Which king of England had six wives?
6 Which king of England was executed in 1649?

156 numbers (BEU 227.6)

On which floor would you get the following things? Which floor would it be if you were in an American department store?

1 a tie
2 writing paper
3 a tent
4 a handbag
5 a lamp
6 a plastic bowl
7 a tennis racket
8 a pair of jeans
9 a lipstick
10 something to eat

JOHNSON'S of London

Ground	1	2	3
Books & Records	Children's	Carpets	Camping
Cameras	Cosmetics	Fabrics	Electrical
Gift Shop	Furs	Gents' clothing	Furniture
Household goods	Jewellery	Ladies' clothing	Gardening
Leather goods	Shoes		Restaurant
Stationery			Sports

157 numbers (BEU 227.7)

How far is it. . . ? Say your answers aloud.

▶ . . . from New York to London?
It's five thousand, five hundred and thirty-six kilometres from New York to London.

1 . . . from Sydney to Johannesburg?
2 . . . from Tokyo to Buenos Aires?
3 . . . from London to Johannesburg?
4 . . . from New York to Sydney?
5 . . . from London to Tokyo?
6 . . . from Tokyo to New York?
7 . . . from Johannesburg to Buenos Aires?
8 . . . from Sydney to Tokyo?
9 . . . from Buenos Aires to London?

LONDON	London				
NEW YORK	5,536	New York			
BUENOS AIRES	11,129	8,539	Buenos Aires		
JOHANNES-BURG	9,067	12,822	8,109	Johannes-burg	
SYDNEY	17,007	16,003	11,755	11,019	Sydney
TOKYO	9,584	10,869	18,340	13,514	7,812

distances in kilometres

158 numbers (BEU 227.8)

1 Read aloud all the information on the cheque.
2 Write the following amounts in words:
£1,122 £127 £1,201 £2,135 £3,110

3 Draw another cheque and fill it in (you can decide yourself who the cheque is payable to, and how much it is for).

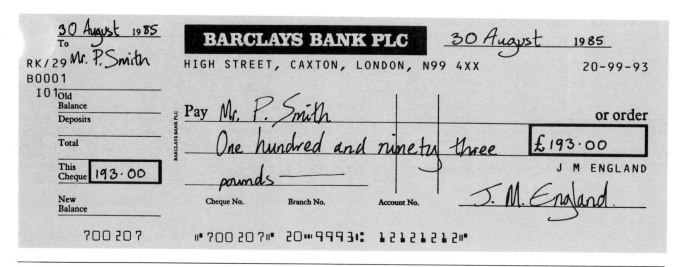

159 numbers (BEU 227.2,3,9)

The table shows the world's four top producers of road vehicles, in millions a year. How many do they make? Read the table aloud.

▶ *Japan produces two point four million lorries a year.*

Japan	2.4 m	4.5 m	3.8 m
USA	2.3 m	6.5 m	
USSR	0.8 m		1.1 m
UK	0.4 m		
France		3.1 m	1.0 m
W. Germany		3.0 m	
Italy			0.8 m

160 numbers (BEU 227.10)

How much do you think they weigh?
Make sentences like this:

▶ *I think X weighs about* _____ *kilos.*

Mary   Julia   Bob   Sally

How tall do you think they are?
Make sentences like this:
▶ *I think X's about* _____ *feet*
_____ *(inches) tall.*

This will help:
2.5 cm = 1 inch
12 inches = 1 foot = about 30 cm

161 numbers (BEU 227.2,12)

▶ *On average, a three-year-old girl is ninety-six centimetres tall and weighs fourteen point five kilos.*

A three-year-old boy weighs fourteen point nine kilos and is ninety-seven centimetres tall.

Now continue to read the table aloud, as in the examples.

Height in cm	Weight in kg	Age	Weight in kg	Height in cm
96	14.5	3	14.9	97
103	16.6	4	16.8	104
111	19.0	5	19.1	111
117	21.0	6	21.2	117
122	23.3	7	24.0	124
129	26.8	8	26.9	130
135	29.8	9	29.6	135
142	34.5	10	33.5	141
154	43.7	12	45.1	156
165	54.3	14	53.5	168

162 **one**: substitute word   (BEU 230)

Which *one*/*ones* would you like?

▶ *I'd like* **the one** *with the stripes/ the striped* **one**/**the one** *on the left etc.*   (1)

1

2

3

4

5

6

7

8

9

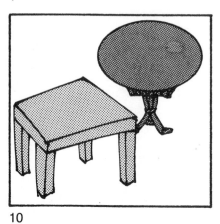

10

11

163 ought (BEU 232)

What *ought/oughtn't* they to do?

▶ I feel awfully tired.
You **ought** to have a sleep/go to bed.
You **oughtn't** to work so hard/to go to bed so late.

1 I don't feel well.
2 I've got a pain in my chest.
3 I think I'm short-sighted.
4 My tooth's aching again.
5 I have to get up very early tomorrow.

6 I'm putting on weight.
7 I lent a friend twenty pounds, but I haven't got it back.
8 My passport has expired.

Write about some more things that you ought to do.

164 ought to have (BEU 232.4)

Name six things that you ought to have done last week.

▶ I **ought to have** written to my uncle.
I **ought to have** repaired my bicycle.

165 own (BEU 233.2)

Complete the sentences, using *of . . . own*.

▶ I usually borrow my brother's car. I can't afford a *car of my own*.

1 Jack shares a room with his brother. He'd rather have a _____ .
2 Mary shares a flat with another student. She'd prefer a _____ .
3 My parents live in a rented house. They'd like to have a _____ .
4 My friend often lends me his pocket calculator. I wish I had one _____ .
5 My sister and her husband have adopted a child. They couldn't have a child _____ .
6 My brother and I are allowed to use our parents' car, but we would both prefer to have a _____ .

7 David smoked my cigarettes all night. He didn't have any _____ .
8 Mark's father pays for all his studies, but Mark would prefer to have money _____ .
9 Aunt Susan always borrows my mother's sewing machine. She hasn't got one _____ .
10 My brother and I sometimes work in a local business. When we have enough money, we're going to open up a _____ .

166 participles used as adjectives (BEU 235)

Complete the sentences, using these adjectives.

~~boring~~	confusing	~~exciting~~
bored	confused	excited
frightening	interesting	~~tiring~~
frightened	interested	~~tired~~

SALLY How did you enjoy the horror film? Was it very __1__ ?
FRED No, not particularly. But then I'd had a hard day, so I was feeling rather __2__ . In fact, I almost fell asleep!
SALLY Really? I'm always __3__ by horror films! Was it at least __4__ ?
FRED Well, I didn't feel very __5__ , not even at the end. We couldn't really understand what was happening. The story was __6__ . Betty was __7__ , too. Anyway, how was the party?
SALLY Well, I'd had a very __8__ day, too, and I didn't meet any __9__ people, so I'm afraid I found it rather __10__ .
FRED Oh, I'm never __11__ at parties. I'm always __12__ in what's going on. Next time, you go to see the film and I'll go to the party!

167 participle clauses (BEU 236)

Rewrite, using a participle clause for the part in italics.

▶ *I didn't know what to do*, so I went home.
Not knowing what to do, I went home.

1 *Because I didn't know* who he was, I didn't speak to him.
2 She sat *and watched* the rain for hours.
3 *I needed some fresh air*, so I went jogging in the woods.
4 *After I had left you*, I went to the post office.
5 *Before you leave on holiday*, always make sure that the doors and windows are locked.
6 *All the people who are queueing over there* are hoping to get tickets for the football match.
7 *If it's properly looked after*, the engine will do another twenty thousand miles at least.
8 *Because he was rich*, he could afford a big house in the country.
9 *I looked at the menu* and found that the prices had gone up again.
10 *I wasn't in a hurry*, so I decided to walk to the office.
11 *He took a taxi* and managed to get to the station on time.
12 Who's that woman *who's talking to the postman*?

168 passive verb forms: simple present (BEU 238)

Name the main country/countries where the following are grown etc. Use the information in the table, and answer as in the examples. If you don't know, guess!

▶ *Cameras* **are manufactured** in the USA and in Japan.
Wheat **is grown** in the USSR and in the USA.

cameras		
coffee		
gold		Australia
maize		Brazil
rice		China
ships		France
silk	build	India
tea	grow	Japan
televisions	manufacture	Malaysia
& radios	mine	the USA
tin	produce	the USSR
wheat		South
wine		Africa
wool		

169 passive verb forms: simple present (BEU 238)

How is bread made? Write out the text, using the following verbs: *cut, deliver, grind, harvest, leave, make, mix, pack, place, put, shape, slice, take* (×2)

In England, most bread *is made* from wheat. When the wheat is ripe, it __1__ . Then it __2__ to the flour mill. At the mill, it __3__ into flour. At the bread factory, first the flour __4__ with fat, salt, water and yeast to make a soft dough. When the dough has risen, it __5__ into pieces and the pieces __6__ into loaves. The loaves __7__ on big trays and __8__ in the oven to bake. After about an hour, the bread __9__ out and __10__ to cool. Then, some of the bread __11__ on a slicing-machine and __12__ into plastic bags. Finally, the bread __13__ to the shops in big vans.

170 passive verb forms: present progressive (BEU 238)

What's being done on the farm?

▶ *The hens **are being fed.*** (1)

Useful verbs: *clean out, collect, dry, feed, harvest, milk, plough, repair.*

1

2

3

4

5

6

7

8

9

10

11

171 passive verb forms: simple past (BEU 238)

When were these famous buildings or monuments
built, begun, completed etc? If you don't know, guess!

▶ *I think the Eiffel Tower **was built** in 1889.* (1)

1 The Eiffel Tower
   1626 or 1889?

2 The Empire State Building, New York
   1930 or 1955?

3 The Colosseum, Rome
   1st Century or 8th Century?

4 The Great Wall of China
   begun 3rd Century BC or 3rd Century AD?

5 The Capitol, Washington
   completed 1665 or 1865?

6 The Pyramids of Gizeh, Egypt
   between 2690 and 2560 BC or 3rd Century BC?

* BC before Christ
  AD after Christ

Now say when some other famous buildings were built.

172 passive verb forms: simple past (BEU 238)

Use an appropriate verb in the passive and match the pairs.
Use *compose, discover, invent, paint, write*.

▶ *'Hamlet'* **was written by** *Shakespeare.*

---

173 passive verb forms: present perfect (BEU 238)

What improvements have been made in your country
over the last fifty years or in your town over the last ten
years? Here are some suggestions. Talk about roads,
hospitals, housing, new laws, schools, the social
system, industry, agriculture, working conditions, the
medical service, public transport, living conditions etc.

▶ *More roads* **have been built**.
The social system **has been improved**.
Compulsory education **has been introduced**.

Useful verbs: *build, develop, improve, introduce,
make, modernize, reorganize, set up.*

174 passive verb forms: future perfect (BEU 238)

What do you think will have been done by the year 2000?
Begin: *I think...* or *I don't think...* Use *find, introduce, invent* and *solve*.

▶ the drug problem
*I don't think the drug problem **will have been solved**.*

talking robots
international traffic laws
a cure for cancer
passenger transport to the moon
a European currency
the world's hunger problems
supersonic trains
new energy sources
the problem of world peace
satellite TV for everyone

175 passive verb forms: 'going to' (BEU 238)

Map 1 shows the town of Litcham as it is now. Map 2 shows the changes that are going to be made. What are these?

▶ *A school **is going to be built** in Wood Street.*

Useful verbs: *build, make bigger, move to, plant, pull down, put up, replace by, turn into, widen.*

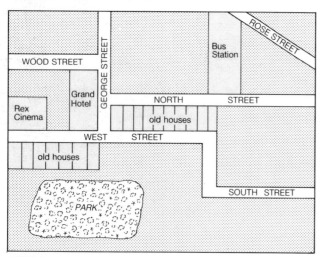

MAP 1

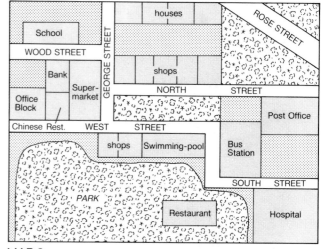

MAP 2

176 past time: simple past (BEU 241)

Put in the past tense of the following verbs, as in the example: *be* (×2), *bring, build, collect, creep, eat, fight, have, hunt, kill, make, play, stay, use.*

About 1¾ million years ago, small groups of people *lived* by the side of a lake in East Africa, now called Olduvai Gorge. We call these people 'homo habilis', which means 'skilful man'. Fossil remains tell us many things about these people, who __1__ our direct ancestors.

They __2__ about 1.5 m tall. They __3__ for their food and __4__ their kill back to their camp.

The hunters __5__ no weapons and probably __6__ up on their prey. They __7__ it with stones or with heavy branches. The hunters __8__ sharp pieces of stone to cut up meat to carry it home. They __9__ the meat raw. They also __10__ tools from stones. Homo habilis __11__ shelters of branches for protection from animals and cold winds.

The women __12__ near the camp with the children. They __13__ eggs, berries and small animals to eat. The children probably __14__ and __15__ as children do today.

177 past time: past progressive (BEU 242)

Imagine you arrived at the scene of the fire in the picture. Say what was happening, what the people were doing, etc.

▶ *Two people **were standing** on the roof.*

178 past time: present perfect simple (BEU 243.3)

What has happened? Say what has
happened in the following pictures.

► **She's won** the
  championship/cup. (1)

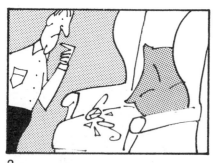

179 past time: present perfect simple (BEU 243.4,5)

Say which of these things
a   you have never done
b   you have already done
c   you haven't done yet
d   you have always wanted to do

speak to a famous person
be on television
have your fortune told
see a James Bold film
see a house on fire
fall in love
win a large sum of money
buy a new car
eat in a famous restaurant
visit London or New York

▶ *I've never spoken* to a famous person.
I've already seen a James Bond film.
I haven't been on television yet.
I've always wanted to visit London or New York.

Write about some other things that you have never done/already done/not done yet/always wanted to do.

---

180 past time: present perfect progressive (BEU 244.2)

What have they all been doing?

▶ *He's been playing* football.   (1)

181 past perfect simple (BEU 245)

Olympic Games 1984

	Day 13		
	G	S	B
USA	63	53	27
Romania	18	14	11
China	15	7	7

	Day 14		
	G	S	B
USA	80	59	30
Romania	20	16	17
W. Germany	17	19	23

	Day 15		
	G	S	B
USA	83	61	30
Romania	20	16	17
W. Germany	17	19	23

The tables show the countries with the most medals on the last three days of the Olympic Games. Compare the tables like this:

▶ 13/Romania/gold
*After day 13, Romania **had won** 18 gold medals.*

1 13/China/gold
2 14/W. Germany/gold
3 13/USA/gold
4 13/USA/silver
5 13/Romania/silver
6 13/China/silver

7 14/USA/gold
8 14/Romania/bronze
9 15/USA/gold
10 15/Romania/gold
11 15/W. Germany/gold
12 15/USA/silver

---

182 possessive 's (BEU 250.1)

Who is who?

▶ Who is Helen?
*She is Jim**'s** wife, Simon and Sally**'s** mother,*
*Hilary and Paul**'s** mother-in-law, the children**'s** grandmother.*

Who is Simon?
Who is Jim?
Who is Paul?
Who is Sally?
Who is Ben?

Helen   **Jim**

Hilary   **Simon**   **Sally**   **Paul**

Susie   **Ben**

183 possessive 's (BEU 250.4)

Whose hat is it?

▶ *Hat number ten is John's.*

Now start with hat number one.

184 possessive 's (BEU 250.4)

Mrs Jones has bought all these things. Which shops
has she been to? There isn't a supermarket in her part
of the town.

▶ *She's been to the butcher's.*

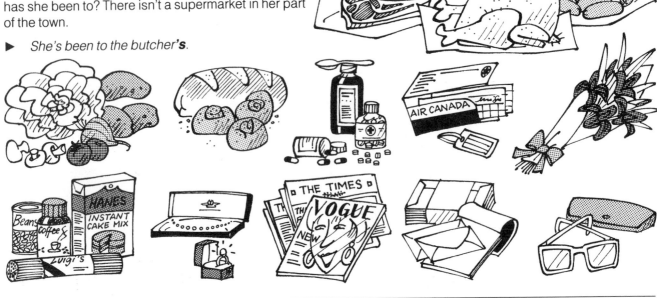

---

185 possessives with determiners (**a friend of mine** etc) (BEU 252)

Kathy and John are cousins. Kathy and Mary are
friends. John and Frank are colleagues. Frank and
Kathy are friends. Kathy and Lucy are neighbours.
Mr & Mrs Hill and Mary are neighbours.

▶ Does John know Kathy?
*Yes, she's a cousin **of his**.*

Who's John?
*He's a cousin **of Kathy's** and a colleague **of Frank's**.*

1 Does Frank know John?
2 Does Mary know the Hills?
3 Does Kathy know Frank?
4 Does Lucy know Kathy?
5 Who's Mary?
6 Who's Frank?
7 Who's Lucy?
8 Who are the Hills?
9 Is Mary a friend of the Hills'?
10 Is Kathy a cousin of Frank's?

---

186 possessives: **mine** etc (BEU 253.2)

Four students share an unfurnished house. They have
all bought some of the furniture and furnishings.
Here's a list of what belongs to whom:

Ann	Charles	Sue and Helen (twins)
fridge	record player	curtains
television	bookshelves	6 chairs
iron	armchair	table
carpets	typewriter	oven
washing machine	radio	kitchen table
cutlery	sofa	cups and saucers
vacuum cleaner	electric kettle	pictures

▶ Does the armchair belong to Charles?
*Yes, it's **his**.*

1 Do the carpets belong to Ann?
2 Does the sofa belong to Charles?
3 Do the pictures belong to the twins?
4 Does the vacuum cleaner belong to Charles?
5 Does the typewriter belong to Ann?
6 Does the record player belong to the twins?
7 Does the radio belong to Charles?
8 Does the table belong to Ann?
9 Do the chairs belong to Charles?
10 Does the television belong to the twins?

187 prepositions at the end of clauses (BEU 257.1 d)

What do you need these things for?

► 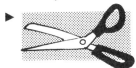 *You need scissors to cut* **with**.

188 present tenses: simple present (BEU 261.2)

Do you do any of these things? Be honest!
Answer as in the examples.

► ... watch rubbish on television?
Yes, I sometimes watch rubbish on television.
No, I never watch rubbish on television.

1 ... drop litter?
2 ... spend too much money on clothes?
3 ... have the radio on too loud?
4 ... neglect your homework/job?
5 ... criticize your teacher/boss behind his/her back?

6 ... tell little white lies?
7 ... ignore a traffic light?
8 ... forget your good manners?
9 ... think more of yourself than of others?
10 ... forget to pay your debts?

189 present tenses: present progressive (BEU 262.2)

What are they all doing?

▶ *Tom is putting up shelves.* (1)

1 Tom

2 Kathy and Mike

3 Sue

4 Jerry

5 Sally and Ben

6 David

7 Jill

8 Barry

9 Diana

190 present tenses: present progressive (BEU 262.2)

An unexpected visitor comes to see you. It's very noisy/very untidy in your house. Explain what's going on. Begin: *'I'm sorry it's so noisy/untidy but... .'* Give as many explanations as you can think of.

▶ *I'm sorry it's so noisy, but **we're having** a party/ but my brother**'s playing** his jazz records.*

*I'm sorry it's so untidy, but **we're moving** the furniture/but **I'm cleaning out** drawers.*

191 progressive tenses with **always** (BEU 263)

What are they always doing?

▶ an absent-minded person **is always forgetting** things.

1	a trouble-maker	6	a gossip
2	an egoist	7	a spoil-sport
3	a clumsy person	8	a pessimist
4	a liar	9	a vain person
5	a hypochondriac	10	a tell-tale

192 questions (BEU 270)

You meet a young American who is staying in your town. You have a lot of questions. Here are the answers. What are the questions?

▶ I come from California.
Where do you come from?
or
Where are you from?

1 I arrived last Sunday.
2 For three weeks.
3 I came by plane and train.
4 At a small hotel in the town.
5 Yes, it's my first time here.

6 Yes, I like it very much.
7 No, I haven't seen that yet.
8 No, I'm afraid I can't speak your language at all.
9 Yes, I do. I like the food very much.
10 No, I haven't been there yet.

193 question tags (BEU 273)

You're speaking to someone you have met for the first time. You have heard several things about him/her from a friend. Find out if it's all true.

▶ He/She is English.
*You're English, **aren't you**?*

You have heard that:

1 He/She is a computer specialist.
2 He/She has been to your country before.
3 He/She is staying for three months.
4 He/She works for an American company.
5 He/She used to work for an English company.

6 He/She knows a few words of your language.
7 He/She would like to learn the language properly.
8 He/She was on holiday in your country last year.
9 He/She doesn't like the food very much.
10 He/She can play tennis very well.

194 reflexive pronouns (BEU 276.2)

Who does it? Answer with *myself*, *yourself* etc, as in the example.

▶ Do you always go to the hairdresser's?
*Yes, I never/hardly ever/cut my hair **myself**.*
*No, I sometimes do/cut my hair **myself**.*

1 Do you iron your own clothes?
2 Does your father/husband have his car repaired at a garage?
3 Do you shop for food yourself?
4 Do you decorate your house/flat yourselves?
5 Do your parents/neighbours clean their house/flat themselves?

6 Do you wash your clothes yourself?
7 Does your mother/wife/girlfriend go to the hairdresser's?
8 Does your father/husband repair things in the house himself?
9 Do you wash your car yourself/yourselves?
10 Did your mother/wife make the curtains herself?

195 relative pronouns: **who** (BEU 277)

Describe the pupils in this old school photo.

▶ *Jane's the girl **who** was very good at sports.*

196 relative pronouns: **that** (BEU 277.2)

Do you know the answers? Choose from the names in the box. If you don't know, guess!

▶ river/flows from Switzerland to the Netherlands?
*The river **that** flows from Switzerland to the Netherlands is the Rhine.*

Sri Lanka	Singapore	USSR
Venezuela	Hong Kong	San Marino
India	Brasilia	Canada
Iceland	Monaco	Rio de Janeiro
Greenland	Peru	

1 tiny country/lies in the middle of Italy?
2 part of China/is leased to Britain until 1997?
3 Danish island/lies in the Arctic?
4 country/has more coastline than any other country?
5 city/has the world's largest football stadium?
6 island/lies at the southern point of India?
7 country/has the highest waterfall in the world?
8 country/covers a sixth of all the land in the world?
9 city/was built specially to be a new capital, about 30 years ago?
10 country/has the most languages?

197 relatives: **whose** (BEU 279)

You want to know who these people are. Begin: *Who's the man whose. . . ?*

▶ *Who's the man **whose** trousers are too big for him?*

Continue. . .

198 relatives: identifying clauses (BEU 280)

Describe the rooms in a house. Say what you do in them. Leave out the relative pronoun, as in the examples.

▶ the bedroom
The bedroom is the room/place you sleep in.

1	the bathroom	6	the nursery
2	the dining room	7	the guest room
3	the kitchen	8	the attic
4	the sitting room	9	the cellar
5	the study	10	the garage

199 reported speech: tenses (BEU 283.3)

Mary B., age 14, wrote this letter to a women's magazine. What did she write/say?

▶ *She wrote that she was 14 and felt confused as to when she became an adult.*

Continue...

I am 14 and feel confused as to when I become an adult. I can get married at 16, but I can't vote until I'm 18! At the cinema I already pay for an adult ticket, but I'm not allowed to see adult films! I can drive a car at 17, but on the bus and tube I start paying adult fares at 15! Travel companies and many airlines offer reductions for children under 12. The age when I become an adult seems to depend on where I'm sitting!

Mary B., London SE3

200 reported speech: tenses (BEU 283.3)

In many countries, it has become compulsory to wear car seat-belts. Many people are for this, some are against it. Here are some opinions. What did they all say?

▶ *Pat Swindon said that she was glad....*

Continue...

Pat Swindon, 26, secretary:
'I'm glad that seat-belts have become compulsory. I'm sure that the number of road deaths will drop.'

Bill Brown, 19, apprentice:
'I hate wearing a seat-belt. I don't feel free. I don't intend to use it in future. I just hope that I don't get caught by the police.'

Patrick Marshall, 30, computer specialist:
'I'm in favour of wearing seat-belts. I always fasten mine. I always did and I always will do.'

Jane Wilson, 24, nurse:
'I see what terrible accidents happen to people who don't wear seat-belts. I hope that belts for the back seats will also become compulsory.'

201 reported speech: questions (BEU 284)

What do they want to know?

▶ *Doris G. wants to know how much notice she must give.*

Continue...

Doris G.

Dear Sue,
I want to leave my present job as a typist. How much notice must I give? I have

Pam E. Surrey

Dear Sue,
How can I get my boyfriend to stop smoking? He never

John K.

Dear Sue,
Should I tell my teacher that I've fallen in love with her? I know it would ca... but I feel u...

David B.

Dear Sue,
When can I legally leave home? I can't possibly

Barry G.

Dear Sue,
Why does my girlfriend tell me lies? My problem ... the fact that

Kathy P.

Dear Sue,
Should I marry a man who's thirty years older than me? ...nst worried about ...in years

Mary M.

Dear Sue
How can I get rid of my spots? I have been to

Roger A.

Dear Sue,
Why haven't I made any friends at my new school? I am friendl... so l...

Lucy L.

Dear Sue,
Why do people treat me like a child? I'm 16 years old and I have just got

Patricia H.

Dear Sue,
My boss has invited me to a party. Should I go? The party will be

Diane B.

Dear Sue,
I have broken my engagement. Do I have to give back my engagement ring?

SUE'S PROBLEM PAGE

202 reported speech: questions (BEU 284)

What does he want to know?

▶   *He wants to know where snow comes from.*   (1)

Continue...

1

2

3

4

5

6

7

8

9

10

11

203 reported speech: orders, requests, advice etc (BEU 285)

What would you advise them to do? Use *advise*, *tell* or *ask*.

▶ Your brother is always having trouble with his old car.
*I would **advise him to buy** a new one.*
Your mother is worried about your future.
*I would **tell her not to worry**.*

1 A friend has a terrible smoker's cough.
2 Your colleague gets very little fresh air and exercise.
3 Your mother looks tired.
4 A man on the phone speaks unclearly. You can't understand him.

5 Your sister is playing loud music. You can't concentrate on your work.
6 Your mother bought some meat that doesn't seem fresh.
7 The waitress in a restaurant has overcharged you.
8 Some children are making a lot of noise. You can't sleep and you feel ill.
9 Your colleague is overworked and needs a rest.
10 Your girlfriend has found a purse full of money on a bus.

204 the same (BEU 288)

Compare yourself with a friend/brother/sister. Here are some ideas: age, height, weight, colour, school, class, town/village, street, house, interests, hobbies, sports, clothes, friends, pop groups etc.

▶ *She has **the same** colour eyes as I have.*
*We live in **the same** street.*
*She doesn't like **the same** pop groups as I do.*

205 shall (BEU 292.2)

What offers of help would you make in these situations?
Begin with *Shall I . . . ?*

▶ ***Shall I** show you the way?* (1)

1   2   3   4

5   6   7   8

206 short answers (BEU 293.1)

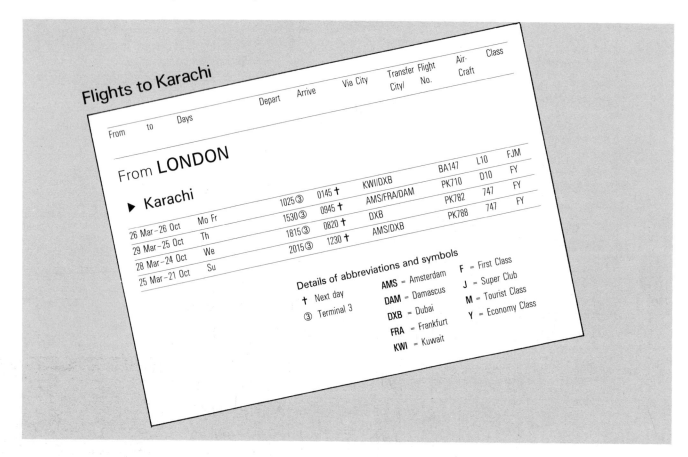

From	to	Days	Depart	Arrive	Via City	Transfer City/	Flight No.	Air-Craft	Class
From LONDON									
▶ Karachi							BA147	L10	FJM
26 Mar – 26 Oct		Mo Fr	1025③	0145 †	KWI/DXB		PK710	D10	FY
29 Mar – 25 Oct		Th	1530③	0945 †	AMS/FRA/DAM		PK782	747	FY
28 Mar – 24 Oct		We	1815③	0820 †	DXB		PK788	747	FY
25 Mar – 21 Oct		Su	2015③	1230 †	AMS/DXB				

Details of abbreviations and symbols

† Next day
③ Terminal 3

AMS = Amsterdam	**F** = First Class		
DAM = Damascus	**J** = Super Club		
DXB = Dubai	**M** = Tourist Class		
FRA = Frankfurt	**Y** = Economy Class		
KWI = Kuwait			

▶ Do all flights go via Dubai?
No, they don't.

Is there a flight on Wednesday?
Yes, there is.

1 Do all flights depart from Terminal 3?
2 Are there any non-stop flights?
3 Does the Sunday flight go via Kuwait?
4 Do the 747 flights go via Dubai?
5 Has flight BA147 got a Super Club class?
6 Is there a flight that leaves in the morning?
7 Does the British Airways flight go twice a week?

8 Is there a flight on Tuesday?
9 Have the Pakistan International flights all got an Economy class?
10 Is there a Pakistan International flight via Frankfurt?
11 Do all flights arrive on the next day?
12 Is there a daily flight?

207 short answers (BEU 293.2)

Give short answers in reply to these statements.

▶ You've got dark hair.
Yes, I have. No, I haven't.

1 You're over 18.
2 You've got brown eyes.
3 You like school/work.
4 You've got long hair.
5 You speak English.

6 You usually get up late.
7 You're shy.
8 You're wearing jeans.
9 You went out last night.
10 You were late for school/work this morning.

208 should (BEU 294)

Several things are in the wrong rooms. Where should they be?

▶ *The fridge* **shouldn't** *be in the bathroom. It* **should** *be in the kitchen.*

Continue. . .

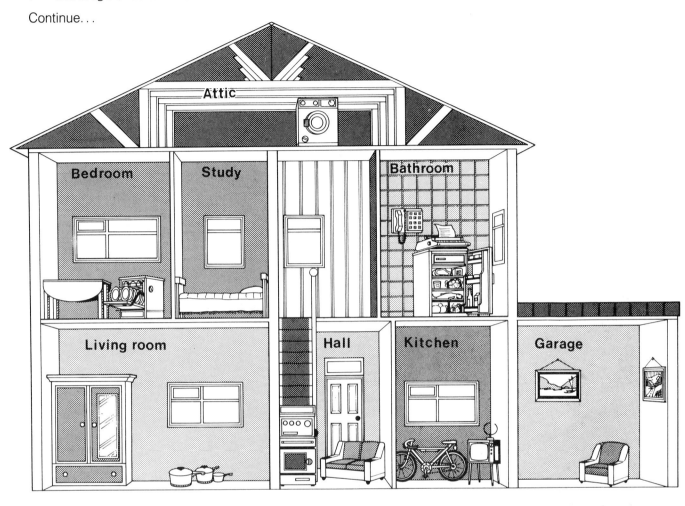

209 should (BEU 294.2)

Use *should* and *shouldn't*. What would you say to a friend who. . .

1 eats too many sweets?
2 has lost his wallet?
3 has an old car that's always being repaired?
4 is too fat?
5 spends too much money on clothes?
6 has lost his job?
7 has got a girlfriend that spends all his money?
8 has bought a record that's scratched?

What advice could your friends give <u>you</u>?

210 **since** (conjunction of time): tenses (BEU 300)

Answer with *since* and the present perfect or past tense.

▶ How long have you known your best friend?
  *I've known my best friend **since** we were at school.*

  How long have you known your neighbours?
  *I've known my neighbours **since** I've been in this street.*

1 How long have you known your best friend?
2 How long have you known your neighbours?
3 How long have you known your best friend's family?
4 How long have you known your class teacher/boss?
5 How long have you known your English teacher?

6 How long have you known your boyfriend/girlfriend/partner?
7 How long have you known your doctor?
8 How long have you known your dentist?
9 How long have you known your butcher?

211 spelling of plural nouns (BEU 301)

What was on the shopping list? Fill in the missing words.

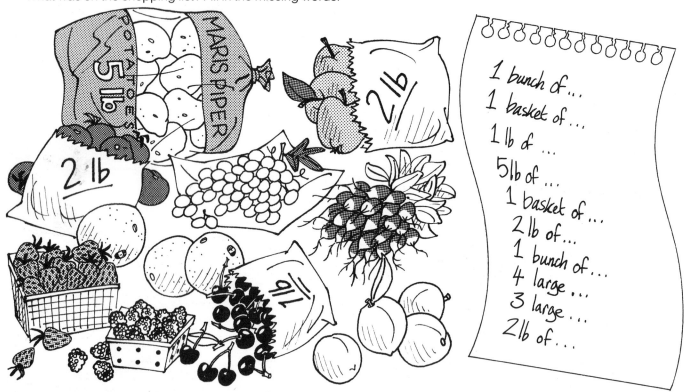

1 bunch of . . .
1 basket of . . .
1 lb of . . .
5 lb of . . .
1 basket of . . .
2 lb of . . .
1 bunch of . . .
4 large . . .
3 large . . .
2 lb of . . .

212 **so** and **not** with **hope**, **believe** etc (BEU 311)

Give suitable short answers with *so* and *not*. Use *be afraid, believe, expect, hope, suppose, think.*

▶ Are you a good cook?
  *I think **so**./I suppose **so**./I hope **so**./I'm afraid **not**.*

1 Are you reliable?
2 Are you a bad loser?
3 Are you overanxious?
4 Are you vain?
5 Are you a bore?
6 Do people enjoy your company?
7 Are you a good singer?

8 Are you a good friend to have?
9 Are you a careful person?
10 Do people complain about you for any reason?
11 Are you successful?
12 Have you got all these answers right?

213 so am I, so do I etc (BEU 312)

Study the application forms and compare the candidates.

▶ *Mary lives in Manchester.* **So does** *Diana.*
  Diana has five O-levels. **So have** *Mary and Susan.*

Application Form
Name: *Diana Clark*
Address: *2, Park Road, Manchester*
Date of birth: *23 July 1964*
Country of birth: *England*
Qualifications: *Maths, History, Geography, English, French (O-levels)*
Shorthand: *100 words per minute*
Typing: *50 words per minute*
Experience: *4 years shorthand typist*
Hobbies: *Cooking, Reading*
Sports: *Tennis, Squash*

Application Form
Name: *Mary Jones*
Address: *14 Hill Street, Manchester*
Date of birth: *30 September 1965*
Country of birth: *Scotland*
Qualifications: *O-Levels: English, Maths, Music, Geography, French*
Shorthand: *120 words per minute*
Typing: *50 words per minute*
Experience: *3 years junior secretary*
Hobbies: *Music, Reading, Dancing*
Sports: *Swimming, Climbing*

Application Form
Name: *Susan Higgins*
Address: *122, Mill Road, Liverpool*
Date of birth: *1 July 1964*
Country of birth: *Scotland*
Qualifications: *O Levels in English, Maths, Biology, French, Art*
Shorthand: *100 words per minute*
Typing: *40 words per minute*
Experience: *Shorthand typist 4 years*
Hobbies: *Dancing, Reading, Cooking*
Sports: *Swimming, Tennis*

---

214 some and any (BEU 314)

What's left after the party? Begin: *There's* **some**. . .,
There isn't **any**. . ., *There's* **hardly any**. . .,
There aren't **any**. . ., *There are* **hardly any**. . .

▶ *There's* **some** *coffee.*

215 somebody and anybody, something and anything etc (BEU 317)

Put in *somebody, something, somewhere, anybody, anything, anywhere*.

1 'Where's the dog? I can't find him _____ .'
   'Well, he must be _____ . Look down the road.'
2 'There's _____ called Smith on the phone for you.'
   'Smith? I don't know _____ by that name.'
3 'I'm going into town today. Is there _____ I can get for you?'
   'No, thanks. I don't need _____ .'
4 I'm looking for _____ , but I can't find it _____ .

5 'Do you know _____ about education in China?'
   'No, not much.'
6 _____ has taken my raincoat by mistake.
7 Let's go _____ nice on Sunday, shall we?
8 'Where did you find this lovely old lamp?' 'In an antique shop _____ in Portland Road.'
9 I'm doing a crossword puzzle. Does _____ want to help me?
10 Have you been _____ exciting this week?

216 still, yet and already (BEU 330)

still, yet or *already*?

1 'Has the postman been _____ ?' 'No, he's _____ chatting to the neighbour.'
2 You needn't wash the dishes. I've _____ done them.
3 'Has it stopped raining _____ ?' 'No, not _____ .
4 'I'm going to Bangkok next month.' 'Oh, you'll enjoy it. I've _____ been there.'
5 'Have you finished your homework _____ ?' 'No, I'm _____ doing it.'

6 She's _____ arrived. The train was early.
7 'Where's John? Has he _____ left?' 'No, not _____ . He's _____ in his office.'
8 He's _____ left Caracas but he hasn't reached Quito _____ .
9 'Have you finished your report _____ ?', 'No, I'm _____ writing it, I'm afraid.'
10 I haven't done the housework _____ . I'm _____ writing letters.

217 subject and object forms (BEU 331.1)

Who likes whom?

▶ *I like Jeff, but he doesn't like me.*

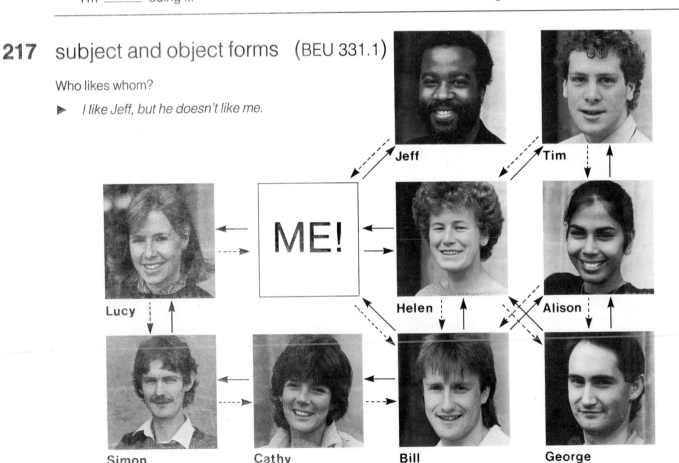

Jeff Tim

ME!

Lucy Helen Alison

Simon Cathy Bill George

218 **such** and **so** (BEU 334)

such or *so*?

1 He's _____ a nice person. I'm sure you'll like him.
2 She's _____ stubborn. She never takes advice from anyone.
3 I really enjoyed the play. It was _____ a good performance.
4 She's not pretty, but she's got _____ lovely eyes.
5 Don't have dinner there. They serve _____ bad food that you can't eat it.

6 Our teacher's very nice. He's got _____ patience.
7 The box is _____ heavy that I can hardly lift it.
8 The countryside is _____ beautiful here!
9 The book's _____ exciting that I can't put it down!
10 He's _____ clever. He knows the answer to everything!

219 **take** (time) (BEU 338)

How long does it usually take you to do the following?

▶ to do the shopping?
  *It **takes** me about an hour.*
  *It sometimes **takes** ages!*
  *It doesn't usually **take** long.*

1 to get to school/work?
2 to write a letter in English?
3 to walk/run a kilometre?
4 to clean your car/bicycle?
5 to clean your shoes?

How long did the following take (you)?

▶ the above sentences?
  *They didn't **take** long.*
  *They **took** me ages!*
  *They **took** me about 5 minutes.*

6 the journey/walk to school/work this morning?
7 the last exercise you did from this book?
8 breakfast this morning?
9 your morning shower/bath?
10 to learn to pronounce English well?

220 telling the time (BEU 342.1,2)

What time do you usually do the following?

▶ get up during the week?
  I usually get up at half past seven (seven thirty) during the week.

1 get up during the week?
2 get up on Sundays?
3 go to bed during the week?
4 go to bed at the weekend?
5 have breakfast?

6 leave home in the morning?
7 arrive home from school/work?
8 have lunch on Sunday?
9 have your evening meal?
10 watch the news on television?

221 **there is** (BEU 345.1)

What is there where? Ask questions and answer them, as in the examples.

pandas	oil	windmills
tea	diamonds	pyramids
coffee	iron	penguins
kangaroos	kiwis	rice
polar bears	alligators	wheat

▶ penguins/the Arctic?
  Are there penguins in the Arctic?
  No, there aren't, but there are polar bears in the Arctic.

rice/Britain?
  Is there rice in Britain?
  No, there isn't, but there's wheat in Britain.

1 windmills/Egypt?
2 kiwis/China?
3 kangaroos/River Amazon?
4 tea/Brazil?
5 pyramids/Holland?

6 iron/Iran?
7 diamonds/Sweden?
8 alligators/Australia?
9 pandas/New Zealand?
10 oil/South Africa?

222 **until** and **by** (BEU 351); **until** and **to** (BEU 352)

until, by or *to*?

1. I'd like to stay _____ Monday, if that's OK.
2. If you want to catch the 3.30 train, you'll have to leave the house _____ 3 o'clock at the latest.
3. We waited _____ half past eight, but he didn't come.
4. The garage mechanic said he could have the car finished _____ Thursday.
5. 'How far did you walk?' '_____ the river and back.'
6. How long is it _____ Christmas?
7. I only work from nine _____ two on Fridays.
8. We're getting up very early tomorrow, so we'll have to be in bed _____ 9 o'clock tonight.
9. Can you wait _____ I come back? I'll only be 5 minutes.
10. The television's broken. We hoped to have it back _____ the weekend, but the shop said they'd have to keep it _____ Wednesday.

223 **used to** + infinitive (BEU 353)

What did there use to be? Compare the plans like this:

▶ There **used to be** a cinema in Duke Street. Now it's a supermarket.
There **didn't use to be** a bus stop in Church Street.

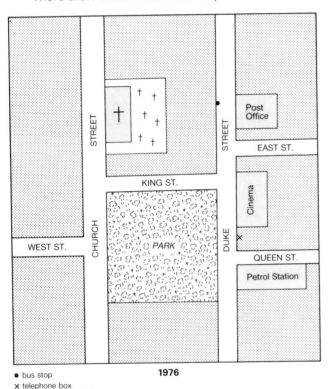

1976

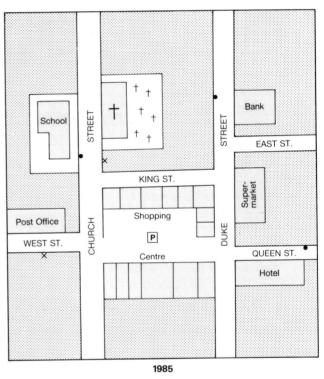

1985

● bus stop
✕ telephone box

224 **(be) used to** + . . .-ing (BEU 354)

Which of these things are you used to doing, and which are you not used to doing?

▶ I'm **used to** getting up early.
I'm **not used to** driving long distances.

working hard	living in a big city
going to bed late	spending a lot of time alone
getting up early	lying in the sun for hours
eating spicy foods	travelling abroad a lot
walking long distances	looking after small children
driving long distances	riding a bicycle

225 verbs with two objects (BEU 356.1)

Say what you *bought*, *gave*, *made* or *sent* different people for recent birthdays and special occasions.

▶ *I bought my friend a record for his birthday.*
I made my little sister a wooden doll for Christmas.

226 **when** and **if** (BEU 360); **whether** and **if** (BEU 361)

when or *if* (or both)? *whether* or *if* (or both)?

1 I'm going to town this afternoon. _____ I see a chemist's, I'll get you some aspirins.
2 I'll see you on the 6.30 bus – _____ I get up early enough!
3 I'm going to Bristol in the morning. I'll ring you _____ I get there.
4 We discussed _____ or not we should agree to the plan.
5 Perhaps I'll fly to Caracas in the autumn. _____ I do, I'll visit you.
6 Ask him _____ he wants to come with us.
7 Please let me know _____ you are coming on Friday or not.
8 _____ you boil water, it turns to steam.
9 _____ you know the answer, say so; _____ not, just keep quiet and hope you won't get asked!
10 _____ I go to London next time, I'll stay at a better hotel.

227 **whoever**, **whatever**, **whichever**, **however**, **whenever**, **wherever** (BEU 365)

Put in whichever is suitable.

1 _____ you do, don't give him the money!
2 'When do you want me to come?' '_____ you like!'
3 You'll enjoy Austria. It's lovely _____ you go.
4 'Which is my seat?' 'You can sit _____ you like.'
5 _____ answers the phone, tell them I'm not here!
6 He'll never be clever, _____ hard he works.
7 'You can take _____ books you like.' 'I don't need any of them.'
8 _____ I see a plane, I always feel like going on holiday!
9 He takes his little brother with him _____ he goes.
10 Please say I'm out, _____ asks for me!

228 **wish** (BEU 367.2)

Kate and Paul have regrets. What do they wish?

▶ *Kate **wishes** she didn't smoke. Paul **wishes** he had gone to university.*

Continue...

```
I smoke.
I've bought so many new clothes.
I can't handle money.
I don't speak a foreign language.
I wasted too much time at school.
I've spent all my savings.
I don't take life seriously.
I haven't got a steady boyfriend.
Paul didn't ask me out.
```

```
I didn't go to university.
I didn't become a teacher.
I didn't work hard enough at school.
I haven't got a car.
I can't dance.
I'm shy.
I don't make friends easily.
I'm not interested in sport.
I didn't dare to ask Kate out.
```

229 worth . . .-ing (BEU 368)

What is it worth doing? Add comments using *worth . . .-ing* with a suitable verb, as in the examples.

▶ Vienna is a beautiful city. *It's worth visiting.*
This radio's broken. *It isn't worth repairing.*

1 'Dr Zhivago' is a good film.
2 These old shoes are shabby.
3 British stamps are very attractive.
4 This old book may be valuable.
5 'Gone with the Wind' is an interesting book.
6 Second-hand TV sets often break down.
7 China is a very interesting country.
8 A good education is important.
9 These old letters and postcards are no good.
10 This is a good record.

230 would rather (BEU 370.2)

You would prefer your girlfriend/boyfriend/husband/wife to do or not to do the following things. Begin with *I'd rather. . .* , as in the examples.

▶ You would prefer him/her to save more money.
I'd rather you saved more money.

You would prefer him/her not to smoke.
I'd rather you didn't smoke.

You would prefer him/her. . .

1 to take life more seriously
2 not to wear old jeans all the time
3 not to buy you so many presents
4 not to work on Saturdays
5 to have his/her hair cut
6 not to drive so fast
7 not to criticize your friends
8 to stop spending money on clothes
9 not to waste so much time on the phone
10 to work a bit harder